Paul Lynde:
A Biography
His Life, His Love(s) & His Laughter

CATHY (FITZGIBBON) RUDOLPH
WITH A FOREWORD BY PETER MARSHALL

Published in the USA by:
BearManor Media
PO Box 1129
Duncan, Oklahoma 73534-1129
www.bearmanormedia.com

ISBN 978-1-59393-743-0

Printed in the United States of America.
Cover photography by Daphne Welds Nichols.
Book design by Brian Pearce | Red Jacket Press.

Table of Contents

This book is dedicated to Paul Lynde, who opened his heart to me, an ordinary girl, and made me feel like the star.

And to my charming and generous dad, who escorted me on my first adventures with Paul. And to my loving mom, a true steel magnolia, who always believed in my writing.

And for my sweet Haley and kind Ryan, who were patient and helpful while I wrote this book. I am beyond blessed and privileged to have you as my children.

And to God, for aligning the stars just right so Paul and I would meet.

I love you with all my heart and soul.

Original host of *Hollywood Squares* Peter Marshall with Paul Lynde. COURTESY
NBC/PHOTOFEST

Foreword BY PETER MARSHALL

There has been much written about Paul and some has been very amusing; but nothing has captured his essence quite like Cathy Rudolph has. She was a fan who became a friend and a confidante to Paul, and she really got to know the guy. Paul was an enigma. His likes and dislikes were acute. I enjoyed this biography immensely. She unveiled things about Paul that I never knew.

This book will appeal to anyone who has ever dreamed of meeting their idol and forming a relationship with them. It is entertaining and yet poignant. For the first time ever, you will really get to know the heart and soul of the man voted America's Favorite Comedian: Paul Lynde.

Hats off to Cathy Rudolph!

My Dream Come True: How I Met Paul Lynde

"How dare that book do that!" PAUL LYNDE

When I was seventeen years old, I had only one mission in my life: to meet Paul Lynde. I had taken down my Donny Osmond posters two years earlier and had replaced them with the funniest and most handsome man I ever saw: Paul Lynde. I loved him best on *The Hollywood Squares*. There was something about his voice and humor that made me laugh more than anyone ever has. I loved the way he laughed, his wink, the mischievous look in his eyes when he said something kinky or dirty — like his answer to the following: "If the right part comes along, would George C. Scott pose nude?" Paul answered, "You mean he doesn't have the right part?" I had never seen or heard anyone who acted the way he did. I was just so attracted to everything about him. My crush on Paul intensified. I had to meet him. I prayed to God every day for this. I was so determined that I bet my high school teachers that this would happen before I graduated.

Nothing short of a miracle could explain what happened next. It was November 17, 1975 and I was in my hometown library in Levittown, Long Island, doing research on Paul. I came across a reference book of Broadway stars and it had a telephone number that said it was Paul Lynde's business number. As soon as I got home, I called the number (Los Angeles, California) and I nearly collapsed when the man who answered was Paul Lynde. It turned out to be his HOME number!!!!

I said, "Paul Lynde?"

He said, "Yes?"

"This is Cathy Fitzgibbon. I am such a big fan of yours. I can't believe I am talking to you!"

"How did you get my home number?" he asked suspiciously. I explained one of the books at my home town library said it was his business number.

He said, "No, it's my home number. It's supposed to be unlisted. How dare that book do that!" I laughed and told him how I admired him and thought he was so funny and talented. I asked about his upcoming shows and was surprised that he was answering all my questions and didn't hang up. The conversation was flowing and I was on cloud nine. I was talking so fast, words spilled out of me, barely letting him get a word in. I don't know what I was thinking back then, but I boldly blurted out:

"I know I'm asking a lot, but would you go to my senior prom with me?"

He said very seriously, "Yes, you're asking a lot."

I said, "No way?"

"Oh, no WAAAAY," he answered in his famous nasal twang, laughing.

So I asked if he would want to meet me, and he gently said, "No dear, do you understand? I can't, if I did I would have to do that for all my fans. It's an absolute almost impossibility."

"Yeah," I said sadly, and then I asked him about his dog Harry MacAfee and he told me the dog had something on his paw and had to get an operation. I continued asking questions about his career. I asked Paul if he ever came to New York and he said yes. So I persisted:

"When are you gonna go, cause, like, you mean more to me than anybody in the world and I'd really want to meet you…and I'm seventeen and I have gone so far out to try to meet you. I would have my father take me." Then there was the first silent moment. I held my breath.

"Well," Paul said very hesitantly, "I may be there Thanksgiving time, and uh, well, the only thing you can do is come by and say hello."

I couldn't believe this was happening. He told me to call him at the Pierre Hotel the week of the twenty-first and he would set something up. I thanked him and hung up. I screamed!

I called the Pierre Hotel on November 22 — this time trying to sound much calmer. He answered.

I said, "Hello, Mr. Lynde, this is Cathy Fitzgibbon."

He said, "Oh hi, Cathy."

"Did you get the get-well card I sent for Harry [his dog]?" I asked.

"Yes, I did and thank you. Harry's doing much better now."

Then I rambled, "Remember you said I could meet you for a picture and an autograph? Well, when would be a good time?"

He asked me how far I was from the city and if I had school. I said I didn't have to go to school, and he said, "No, you go to school." We arranged to meet at three in the afternoon. I did not go to school that day. I was way too excited.

On November 24, 1975, I took the train with my dad to New York City. I was wearing a new skirt and blouse and trying not to throw up all over it. We stepped out of the train, and the cold air helped ease the tsunami in my stomach. I held tight to the red rose I carried for Paul, and we headed to the Pierre Hotel. I waited anxiously in the lobby, holding the rose in my shaky hands.

The hotel was on fire! No one was allowed to go up or down. I was so nervous I would not get to meet the man of my dreams. Firemen were running through the lobby with long hoses, alarms were going off, and it was chaos. I had someone at the front desk ring Paul's room. There was no answer. My heart sank.

"Cathy I think we should get out of the building," my dad said.

"There is no way I am leaving," I said emphatically.

I glanced at my watch. It was a little after three. I scanned the lobby, looking at every man not wearing a fireman's uniform. I looked over at the elevators hoping he would step out of one, but they were now off limits. People were still going in and out of the hotel. I looked back toward the lobby at the revolving doors. That's when I saw him! He was walking into the lobby. He was taller than I expected, almost six feet. He was wearing a navy blue shirt, dark jacket, and slacks. His face was tan, his sandy brown hair looked soft and it was a little windblown to the side. My heart was racing. He looked even better than I thought he would in person.

I left my dad, approached Paul, and held out the red rose. "Mr. Lynde, I'm Cathy Fitzgibbon."

He said hello and took the rose with a smile. "I am running so late," he said. "I went to the chiropractor and the taxi was stuck in traffic and I wanted to shower before I met you." I told him he looked great. He seemed flattered. He walked over to the front desk and I followed. He asked for his messages and then handed them to me to read, explaining he didn't have his reading glasses with him. I was so nervous I don't even remember what I read to him or who they were from, but I felt honored to do this.

Paul wanted to take us up to his suite, but a hotel worker told Paul that he couldn't go up there right now, as there was a fire on one of the floors. So Paul said, "Let's get a drink down here. Go get your dad."

I motioned to my dad, who was still in the lobby, to come over. I introduced him as Jerry Fitzgibbon. They shook hands and Paul said, "Boy, you really are fans. You stood waiting for me in the smoke and the flames and with the entire fire department running around." My dad burst out laughing. We followed this great celebrity into a dining area in the hotel. The host stopped Paul and said, "I'm sorry, house rules; I can't let you in without a tie and jacket."

"How can I get a tie when the hotel is on fire and they won't let me up to my suite?" Paul asked him, sounding annoyed. Then he turned to me

"Our Afternoon at the Sherry." Paul Lynde and Cathy (Fitzgibbon) Rudolph (November 24, 1975). COURTESY OF JERRY FITZGIBBON

and my dad and said, "Let's go down to the Sherry Netherlands." So there I was, with my dad, walking the streets of New York with Paul Lynde. He told us how he loved New York and the people in it, and what a great city it truly was. I wondered how the crowds of people didn't notice it was Paul Lynde walking past them.

We arrived and were seated at a table by the window. I immediately noticed that every single table in the room had a red rose on it. My dad and I ordered a glass of wine. Paul had vodka and something, and he asked the waiter to bring him an extra glass of water to put my rose in. I took out the page that I had photocopied his phone number from the library and showed him. Paul said, "That's my number." He said it's been in there for years and no one ever called it. Then we talked about his life, career, and all the shows and movies he had done.

He was both witty and serious. He answered every question I asked him and was so polite. He definitely had that movie star air about him, and yet he was so gracious. Paul was not quite the comedian you see on TV; he was more on the quiet side, bordering shy, but every now and then he would do a lower key "Paul Lynde" voice. My dad laughed so hard and I giggled. We were all talking, and soon it felt very comfortable in spite of my nervousness. At one point, Paul asked me what I wanted be when I grew up, and I said, "An author."

Jerry Fitzgibbon, my father, photographer, and escort on my first adventure with Paul. COURTESY OF PATRICIA FITZGIBBON

Paul turned to my dad and asked, "And what does she want from me?"

My dad said, "Nothing. She's just a devoted fan." I think at that moment Paul felt secure. I was not after him for anything. This was so different, I later learned, than what he was used to most of the time.

The conversation lasted almost two hours. At one point, I asked him if he made up the funny answers he gave on *The Hollywood Squares*. He answered so sincerely, "No dear, someone writes them for me."

"Well they are funny anyway," I added smiling.

We talked at length. Then Paul said he had guests arriving and had to get back to the Pierre. I asked him if my dad could take a picture of us and he said, "Sure."

Then he asked me if his hair looked alright and I said, "Perfect."

As my dad got ready to take the photo with his Polaroid camera, Paul said, "Wait, let's make sure the rose is the picture."

When the picture developed, Paul took out his pen and wrote on the back of it: "To Cathy, Our afternoon at the Sherry, Love and Laughter, Paul Lynde." Then he wrote something on a piece of paper. As we stood up to go, Paul said, "Cathy you keep that phone number and here's my address; so if you ever come to LA, you are welcome to visit me at my home."

I couldn't believe what I was hearing. It was beyond what I prayed for. Paul shook hands with my dad, and I asked him if I could give him a kiss on the cheek. He gave a resounding "yes," and I stood on my tiptoes and planted my first kiss. Then Paul picked up the rose, and the three us walked out to the street together. I thanked him for meeting me and my dad and for spending so much time with us. He said he would be back in New York in a few weeks for Christmas and would call and invite me to see him again. I was mesmerized. I met the man of my dreams, this huge star, and now he was forming a friendship with me. I felt like the luckiest person in the entire world. This was just our beginning.

My phone rang on Christmas Eve. My sister, Maureen, answered and she could hardly speak when it was Paul on the other end. I was sleeping off the drinks I had at an office holiday party. My Mom and Maureen were trying to wake me up, "Cathy, Paul Lynde is on the phone," they repeated, shaking me. I raced to the phone in a stupor.

"So how are you?" I asked the man of my dreams. Paul said he was fine and he called because he wanted to wish me, "A great Merry Christmas." I was so surprised. He said he was going to church and then to Liuchow's for dinner.

"So how are you?" I asked again.

"You asked me that already," he said sounding slightly annoyed. Then he invited me to come see him again at the Pierre on the twenty-seventh. "Merry Christmas, Cathy." He said as we were ending the conversation.

"You are my Christmas," I said, and hung up.

Once again I boarded the Long Island railroad with my dad. This time we took my youngest sister, Eileen, along. When we arrived at the hotel, I called Paul in his room, and he told me to come on up. I was nervous and excited. My dad and sister waited in the lobby. I took the elevator up to his suite, all the way wondering if I should shake his hand or give him a kiss. I found his room and knocked. The door opened and my heart did a flip as I was eye level with a mass of chest hair surrounded by gold lions on a black shirt. I looked up into Paul's bright green eyes; he smiled as he leaned down, gave me a warm kiss on my mouth, and hugged me. I couldn't believe how he kissed me and just how happy he was to see me. I walked into the room and was surprised to see other people there. Paul introduced me to Jan and Joel Forbes. He told me Jan went to Northwestern with him and they were lifelong friends.

Then he introduced me to a handsome man named Pablo (an artist from Spain he met in the village). Pablo did not speak much English, and I just assumed he was Paul's secretary. Paul told Jan and her husband Joel how I found his phone number in a library book. He said he was thinking, "Oh my Gooodness! Who is this girl on the phone?" For the next few hours we would all talk, Paul would make jokes with his famous voice, and we would all laugh and just have a really good time. At one point, Paul leaned over to me and said, "Cathy, you have the same ESP with me as Karen Valentine." I wasn't exactly sure what he meant, but I knew he was very fond of her so I felt special hearing this.

A few hours later, my dad and sister came up to the room to tell me it was time to leave. Paul greeted my dad warmly and kidded Eileen about

"Christmas time at the Pierre." Eileen (Fitzgibbon) Ruggerio, Paul Lynde, Cathy (Fitzgibbon) Rudolph. COURTESY OF JERRY FITZGIBBON

what it must be like to be my sister. Then I wanted a picture taken of us, so my Dad popped in a Sylvania flashcube for the camera. At first I didn't include my sister in the photo and Paul called me, "Sellllllllfish." When we finished taking photos, Paul insisted my dad and sister stay a while. He had Pablo get my sister and dad drinks, and we all sat back and talked. After about an hour, my dad stood up and said we were going to head home. I wanted to stay there forever.

Paul shook my dad's hand and kissed my sister on the cheek. He came over to me and held my hands in front of me and then he kissed me on the mouth, this time longer then when he greeted me. I thought I would faint. He spoke from his heart as he wished me a "Very Happy New Year," and said he would call me soon. I felt hypnotized as we walked out. My life was perfect.

In July of 1976, Paul was on tour doing *The Paul Lynde Show* and was coming near my hometown, so my dad bought my family and my friends front row tickets. When Paul arrived, he left a message for me saying that I could meet him at the pool at the Holiday Inn and added, "Have your father take you." I still didn't have a driver's license, and my dad was working that day, so my sister dropped me off. I scanned the lounge chairs and nearly melted when my eyes fixed upon him in a bathing suit with a sun reflector under his chin, followed by a great tanned body.

Paul was very quiet today and serious, so I did most of the talking as he soaked up some rays. When I asked about his show, he told me he couldn't get used to this theater in the round. I jabbered on about my prom, which I had asked him to go with me again, after we met. He said he would have gone with me, but was obligated to tape *The Hollywood Squares* that day. I was honored he actually considered it.

A few hours later, my sister Tricia came to pick me up. This was the first time she would meet Paul. After they said hello, Paul reminded me to come backstage after the show. As we drove home, Tricia told me she hadn't realized how handsome he was and that when she saw him in his bathing suit she almost fell into the pool.

The next night was the show, and Paul swaggered out holding a drink and smoking a cigarette. The audience was already laughing before he even spoke. "Haha, I can smoke and you can't," he teased. He loved menthol cigarettes but they affected his voice, so he stayed away from them. After a while, I noticed that he did not turn to different areas of the audience as a performer would normally do when it's a round stage. He did some monologues and some jokes, and most of the evening, he seemed to direct the whole show toward me. "Excuse me for not turning around, but I've been talking to Cathy Fitzgibbon the whole time," Paul announced. He then told the audience the story of how I found his home phone number in my local library and called him up. "She convinced me to meet her and she is truly a wonderful fan." Then he added, "There are some kids I truly love to love," and he broke out with his signature song, "Kids" from *Bye Bye Birdie*, and he sang it to me.

When the show was over, I immediately went backstage where Paul embraced me. He had drinks for everyone and introduced me to the performers from the show. The room was filled with chatter and laughter, and Paul was "on."

It was time for the star of the show to go out and greet his fans. We walked arm in arm to the table that was set up for him. He signed autographs and had a few more drinks, and I saw the quiet man I had spent the afternoon with the day before become the life of the party. He was as hilarious as we all knew him to be from *Squares*. The crowd loved him. In between penning his "Love and Laughter always," he told the fans, "This is Cathy Fitzgibbon and I love her. She is devoted to me and better looking than the entire Osmond family…and has better teeth."

"Backstage at Westbury Music Fair" (1976). Paul Lynde and Cathy (Fitzgibbon) Rudolph. COURTESY OF JERRY FITZGIBBON

I was in awe of all the attention he was giving me. I was thinking to myself, *Paul's the star, but he's making me feel like one.* As the line was getting down to the last few admirers, I asked him to sign my program. Someone said my name started with a K and Paul said, "No, *my* Cathy starts with a C." As he began to write, he said, "There is only one thing I can write, and it's the words that are perfect for us, and it's the way I feel about Cathy. The Beatles wrote it and it's *Silly Little Love Song*." Then he stood up and sang the lyrics, "I love you…I love you." He told my dad I was going to be a star and told my mom that she was a genius for having me. He called her Mother Aspirin because he said she was going to need them for having me as a daughter. Then he pulled me into his arms, hugged me so tight, and leaned over. And just like Clark Gable did with

Scarlet O'Hara in *Gone With The Wind,* he kissed my mouth with such intensity. It was just after midnight, now the Fourth of July, and boy did I see fireworks. We kissed for a long time, until his bodyguard came and tried to separate us, but neither one of us was letting go.

I was so in the moment that I did not hear my mother yelling to my father, "Jerry, get him off of her, Jerry get him off of her," as my friend, Robin, told me later. Finally, his bodyguard got us apart and turned to me with a disapproving look. "Don't you see what you do to him?" he scowled. I had no idea what he was talking about.

As his bodyguard was steering Paul toward an exit, I ran over to Paul and said, "I will miss you." Paul squeezed my hand and whispered in my ear, "Dear, wherever I go, you will be with me."

Over the next year, Paul and I kept in touch through cards, letters, and phone calls. I had made plans to visit Paul at his home, which my mom now had reservations about, but there was no stopping me. I arrived in Los Angeles on June 23, 1977, with my friends Pam Morrow and Barbara Brinkerhoff. Barbara stayed with her sister, Arlene Kanea, in her apartment on Sepulveda Blvd in Los Angeles, and Pam and I stayed nearby at the cheapest motel we could find. The four of us drove to Beverly Hills, found North Palm Drive, and pulled up into Paul's driveway. Pam noticed there were no windows, and I was surprised how plain and masculine the house looked. It reminded me of pictures I had seen of his previous home, which was also black and white, but this one was much smaller. Paul greeted us, and I introduced my three friends. He led us to his backyard by the pool, and my friends asked him questions about his career and other famous people he knew. He answered cordially but otherwise he did not talk much, except to say that Karen Valentine would love the shirt that Barbara was wearing. When Paul went into his house to get more beverages, Pam whispered to me. "I can't believe how shy he is…and Cathy, I noticed whenever anyone else is talking, he just keeps staring at you. He must feel like a piece of meat because we all want to meet him just because he's famous."

"No," I disagreed, "you are here because you are my friends."

Paul expressed how disappointed he was that his house was not set up for us to see. He had been staying in the guest house on the property and had just recently moved into the main house, but his furniture and décor had not arrived. He gave us a tour of his home, which was filled with boxes, except for his bedroom, which had a chair, a television, a bed, and a dresser. As we passed the dresser, I was elbowed three times by my friends; there, on top, was an eight-by-ten photo of me and Paul that I had sent him a year ago. It was the only photo in the house!

The doorbell rang, and Paul was handed a huge plant with a large red bow on it. Paul read the card: it was from KC, of KC and The Sunshine Band, wishing him good luck in his new home. My friends and I thought it was so cool, as he had so many hit songs out like "Shake Your Booty" and "That's the Way I Like It."

At the end of the day, we thanked Paul for his hospitality and left. I

Paul and Cathy. (This was the photo on Paul's dresser — the only photo in his house.) COURTESY OF JERRY FITZGIBBON

returned the next day to attend a children's benefit in Los Angeles that he had invited me to. There was a limousine waiting for us in the driveway. Paul came out of his house holding a drink and introduced me to his chauffeur, Jonathon. I had been talking away, and Paul said to his chauffeur, "Excuse me Jonathon, would you like me to translate? Cathy talks so fast."

"I don't think she does." Jonathon said.

"OH, you're ble-e-e-ssed," Paul teased. Today he was very funny and more talkative then yesterday. We arrived at the benefit, which was held outside in an open field. We stood with Angie Dickinson, Earl Holliman, Rosy Greer, Dick Martin, Dick Sargent, and Ethel Kennedy. Angie Dickinson was the friendliest, and we spoke for a while. Then she pointed at me and said to a young boy who was near us, "Look, she's with Paul Lynde." I felt important.

As we walked around the open field, Paul said to me, "I always feel safe with you." I wasn't sure what he meant, but I liked how it sounded. I told him that I had picked up a copy of *California Life* when I was at the airport because he was on the cover. I thought he would be happy about it, but instead he became quite upset. He asked if the magazine article mentioned anything about Jim Davidson. I had no idea who he was talking about, but I assured him there was no mention of that name and that it was a very positive article. Paul let out a sigh of relief, put his hand on my arm, and said, "Oh, Cathy it was the most terrible thing that has ever happened to me." I listened as he touched on the story of how his friend had fallen to his death from a hotel window right in front of his eyes. Though it had happened over ten years ago, he was still emotionally affected by it. I had never heard anything about it until that moment. I felt sorry for him.

There were television cameras filming all the stars, and the event was to be aired later that day on a local station. Paul stopped to talk to different people, and I held his shoulder bag as he signed autographs. Towards the end of the afternoon, a scruffy looking man with a gray beard approached Paul and asked him for an interview. Paul gladly spoke into the microphone, answering the man's questions about the benefit for kids and the day's events. Then he asked, "So tell me; what do you think about Anita Bryant?"

Paul became angry, "Why are you harassing me?!" Then he grabbed my arm and said, "Come on Cathy. Let's get away from his man," and we ran. When we were far away from the reporter, he said, "Ya see, I am here for the children and that man just had to ruin it."

I stayed silent, trying to figure out what happened. I had no idea who Anita Bryant was, other than the lady who did the orange juice commercials, or why Paul was so upset. We returned to the limo and headed back to his house. Paul invited Jonathon to come in and watch the benefit on TV with us. I told Paul I wanted to call my parents so they could see us on TV, but Paul said it was only being showed locally. We had about a half hour until we had to leave for Paul's next engagement. The doorbell rang, and a man, who I guess was about thirty years old, came in. Paul introduced Carlo to me, and we all sat and watched the benefit. I was sitting on a chair and, as I leaned down, I spilled my soda all over his new carpet. Paul just said, "No more drinks for you," and he grabbed a towel and cleaned it up. Then he told the story of the rude reporter who questioned him earlier. He mentioned something about a campaign. When he finished, I innocently asked, "What does Anita Bryant have to do with you?"

Paul answered, "She attacked my people." I couldn't believe what he just admitted to me and everyone in the room.

When it was time for us to leave, to head to the Bill Cosby Dog Show, we went back in the limo, and this time Carlo joined us. I was the first one in, and then Carlo sat next to me, followed by Paul. Paul was paying a lot of attention to Carlo, and I was jealous. I also wanted to be sitting

"Cathy's Clown." Paul with Cathy (Fitzgibbon) Rudolph. COURTESY OF BARBARA BRINKERHOFF.

next to "my man." Rock music was playing, and Carlo took out a joint. He hesitated and then looked at Paul, who said, "Light it up." *This* was Hollywood, I thought.

Paul gave me his bag to hold while he went to present an award. Carlo, Jonathon, and I sat eating hotdogs in the bleachers. I wasn't paying attention to the show, I was daydreaming about Paul. A few minutes later, he came back, looking a bit annoyed. "I've been paging you Cathy, didn't you hear me?" I shook my head. "I needed my reading glasses and I wanted you to bring them to me."

"Sorry," I said, and I handed him his glasses. When the show ended, we walked back to the limo. I was still sulking from all the attention Paul was giving Carlo, and I did not hide that fact.

Paul put his arm around me and asked, "What's the matter, Cathy?"

I put my nose in the air and said "Nothing."

He whispered something to Carlo, who then asked me if I wanted to sit next to Paul. "Yes," I said with vindication, and I did.

On the ride back, Paul had his arm around me and I was now content. As we drove through the town, Paul stuck his hand out the limousine's blackened window and shouted, "Look everybody! It's a star's hand!" I was laughing so hard. He then rolled down the window and stuck his head out, shouting, "It's Paul Lynde." People began screaming, they ran over, and he signed autographs for all of them.

As the evening ended, Paul asked me where I wanted to be dropped off. I panicked. I was staying in that run down motel and I did not want him to see that. I remembered Barbara's sister lived on Sepulveda Blvd. I asked Jonathon to drop me off over there. Paul asked, "Is this where you're staying?"

"I'm not sure." I answered.

"You're staying here and you don't even know the address?"

"I didn't sleep here last night," I said.

"OHHHH You got lu-u-u-u-cky!!!" Paul teased, and I playfully slapped him lightly across the face.

"Oh, you struck a star," he half laughed. Then he stepped out of the limo and took my hand to help me out. As I thanked him for a great time, I put my arms round his neck and kissed him. I could hear him chuckling as we exchanged breaths. There I was kissing Paul Lynde on the streets of L.A. — I was stupefied. Then I headed down the block, without a clue to where I was going. It took me over twenty minutes to find Arlene's apartment. When I found it, I opened the door and floated in.

The following spring, in a phone conversation, Paul said he was going on tour to do *The Impossible Years*, but the show would not be coming near my town. I was disappointed, but after we hung up, I decided I would surprise him. I called my friend Barbara, and we flew to Norfolk, Virginia. We arrived on August 5, two days before I would be turning nineteen, and I had my own romantic ideas of how I planned to celebrate it with Paul.

The show had already started at Chrysler Hall when Barbara and I walked into the dark theater that screamed with laughter. I watched Elizabeth Allen and Paul performing on stage. As soon as the show ended, I sent a message backstage, letting Paul know I was there. I waited by the table with a crowd who were lined up to get his autograph. The star of the show had changed his clothes and made an entrance wearing a long leopard caftan. He had a thick gold chain around his neck, a matching bracelet on one wrist, and an expensive watch on the other wrist. The crowd cheered and applauded for him. He then shouted, "Is *my* Cathy with a C here?"

I answered as loud as I could from the back of the crowd, "Yes I am," and I squeezed through the fans with Barbara behind me. Paul and I hugged each other with all our heart.

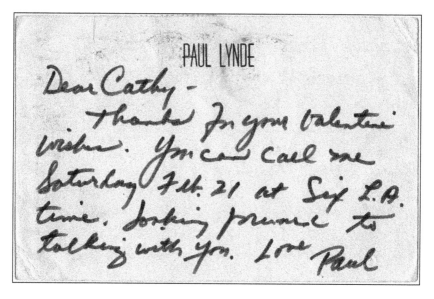

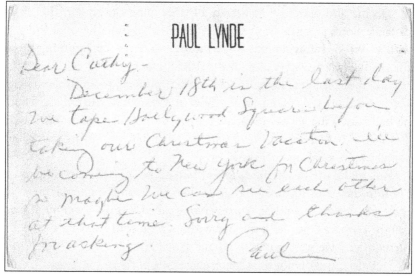

Letters from Paul — Valentine wishes, and *The Hollywood Squares.*

He looked at Barbara and said, "You've changed your hair, Babs. I like it." He introduced me to the crowd and told "our story," of how I found his home phone number in a library book and convinced him to meet me.

He took a seat at the table set up for him and began signing playbills and brochures with his "love and laughter always." We stayed next to him while he signed autographs for the long line of fans. He was joking with

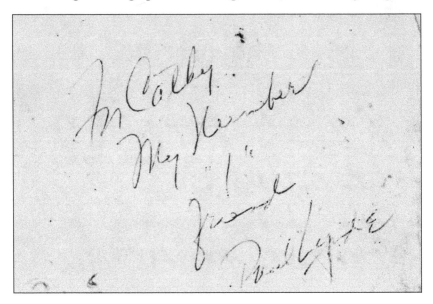

the people and patiently answered all their questions, but with a little distance. Sometimes he was very serious and other times he would answer with a sarcastic funny remark. His wit came out with such lightning speed that he had the crowds falling over with laughter.

When the last person left, I took out two photos of Paul and me from my purse that were taken at his show at Westbury Music Fair, where he had kissed me so passionately. I asked him to sign them. He wrote: *To Cathy, My #1 Fan, My #1 Friend.* I was so touched by his words, but somehow, I was also a little sad.

Paul told Barbara and me to follow him backstage to his dressing room. He introduced us to his costar, Liz Allen, and some other members of the cast. One cast member, who everyone called "Gunk" for some reason, caught Barbara's eye; he hung out with us. Paul told Liz that it was my birthday and we were going to go out dancing.

Paul, Liz, and one of the theater managers got into the limo. Barbara, Gunk, and I followed them to a club nearby. Paul and I walked in together arm in arm. When the crowd inside saw that it was Paul Lynde walking into the club, they went wild. Swarms of fans mobbed him. He loved it and held his head high, snickering along with his famous laugh. I felt like I was walking on the red carpet. One guy in his twenties, who had thick curly blonde hair, literally fell at his feet worshiping him. Paul was polite and tried to keep walking, but the guy wrapped his arms around Paul's leg and wouldn't let go. He was telling Paul how much he loved

Elizabeth Allen, Paul, and Cathy (Fitzgibbon) Rudolph. PHOTO COURTESY OF BARBARA (BOCHICCHIO) BRINKERHOFF

him. Paul smiled politely and took a step forward, but the beach-boy-type guy held on. As Paul tried to walk, the guy was now was being dragged on his stomach. After a few more steps, his friends took hold of him and peeled him off of the star.

The club was mostly men. This was new to me, but I didn't care. I was with Paul Lynde, and I held on tighter to my man. Paul found a table and a Latin-looking waiter arrived. Paul ordered drinks, and the waiter returned so quickly that there was no doubt Paul was king. The music was thriving with great disco tunes. "Let's dance," I said to Paul, and the people parted the way to give us room. It was my first time dancing with the star. He took my hand and twirled me around, did a few hustle steps, and would say things to make me laugh. The fifty-two-year-old had lots of energy, and I was on cloud nine.

A few men came up to us while we danced, trying to cut in, I wasn't sure if they wanted to dance with me or Paul, but the star politely told them he was dancing with me tonight. Later, others approached him, offering whiffs of poppers — also known as butyl nitrate, which was bought over the counter and gave a quick head rush when inhaled. It seemed to be quite popular among the dancers.

The night flew by so fast, and then our waiter stopped by our table again. It was last call, and it was nearly 2 a.m. I was a nervous wreck trying to figure out how the night would end. I wondered where he would take me after this and how much more romantic the night would get. Then the lights flickered, signaling the club was closed. Paul stood up from the table as Liz said good night to us. Then he gave me a kiss, and said, "Good night, Cathy. I will see you tomorrow at the show. Come backstage when it's over." My face fell, as I watched Paul walk out with our waiter.

I was devastated. I grabbed Barbara, and we headed back to our hotel where I cried myself to sleep. The next afternoon, Gunk had invited us over to his hotel to hang out by the pool with him and some other cast members before the show. One of the cast members asked Barbara why I was upset. He couldn't understand why I liked Paul so much and said that Paul got really nasty when he drank, and didn't I know he was gay?

When Barbara told me this, I was angry, and I said, "But he kissed me — a real kiss. He sang, 'I love you,' to me, and remember how his other bodyguard said to me, 'Don't you see what you do to him?' I must mean something to him, otherwise why am I in his life?"

That evening, Barbara and I went to Paul's dressing room after the show. Paul could see I was upset with him. Liz was there and a few other people from the cast. Paul kept asking Barbara, "Where's G-u-u-u-u-nk, Babs?" making everyone laugh at the way he said his name. I kept my attitude until he told everyone in the room how the waiter from the club stole his watch. Then he added, "I know *my* Cathy would never do that."

Somehow, this made me feel better. "Let's go back to the club again," Paul suggested.

As the two of us walked quietly into the club, Paul said to me, "I like your shoes."

"Would you like to borrow them?" I asked in my best sarcasm.

"Smart ass," he responded with a side nod of this head. That seemed to ease the tension between us. We sat at the same table as we had the night before. We had a different waiter tonight — I was relieved. Paul became very quiet. He did not talk much or want to dance tonight.

When the DJ announced the last song for the night, I leaned over and said, "Come on, Paul. It's the last song. Please dance with me."

I heard the first note of Donna Summer's "Last Dance," and Paul stood up, he took my hand, and we slow danced. He held me tight as we danced cheek-to-cheek, and I leaned my head on his shoulder. I was in heaven, and I didn't want the song to end.

The club lights were turned up and we headed out to the limo. It was the last night in town for Barbara and me. The driver dropped us off at Chrysler Hall, where we had our car. Paul helped me out of the limo. I reached up, put my arms around his neck, and gave him a long kiss.

I watched the limo drive away.

Paul with Barbara Bochicchio-Brinkerhoff. COURTESY OF CATHY RUDOLPH

LEFT: "Thumbs Up." Paul and Cathy dancing. RIGHT: "The Last Dance." Paul Lynde and Cathy (Fitzgibbon) Rudolph (1978). COURTESY OF BARBARA (BOCHICCHIO) BRINKERHOFF.

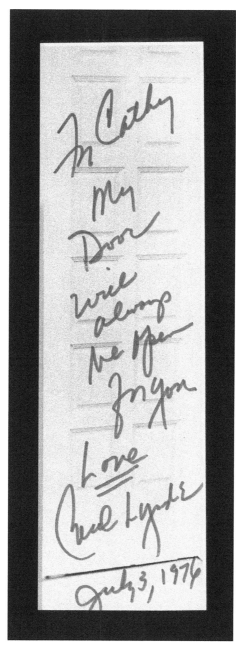

"To Cathy, My Door will always be open for you."

CHAPTER 1

Paul Grew Up in a Prison

Paul Lynde was a guest on the Tonight Show in May, 1976, when Joan Rivers was guest hosting for Johnny Carson. Joan complimented him on how slim he looked. She asked Paul if he was fat as a child.

Paul answered, "I was 260 pounds!"

Joan replied, "At birth?" The audience laughed.

Paul said, "Talk about stretch marks." The audience roared.

Sylvia Bell Doup Lynde was rushed to St. Vincent De Paul's Mercy Hospital, in Mount Vernon, Ohio, on June 13, 1926. She had just given birth in her home, minutes earlier, to her fifth child, Paul Edward. She was in critical condition. Hoy, her husband, arrived rushing through the hospital doors and carrying his newborn son against his chest.

Some of the Catholic nuns, who were also nurses, scurried silently past the worried husband in a blur of starched white caps and uniforms. Sylvia was overweight and she was having serious complications with this birth.

Hoy waited, and he tried to comfort the crying infant boy in his arms. After a while, the doctor appeared and told Hoy that his wife had to remain in the hospital. Hoy nodded, wondering how he would care for his newly born son with four other children at home. The doctor spoke to the nuns. Minutes later, Hoy exited the hospital empty handed.

The Lyndes were Methodist, not Catholic. The nuns agreed to take care of baby Paul at the hospital, while his mother recovered. According to Nancy Noce (Paul's eldest niece), it was an unusual arrangement for that time. Paul was adored by the nuns. They took turns feeding and holding him, and gave him lots of attention; he became the star of Mercy Hospital. Meanwhile, at home, Paul's sisters Grace (who was nine years old) and Helen (who was seven) attended school. Paul's two brothers Richard (six years old) and Coradon (Cordy — who was three) stayed at home, while family, friends, and neighbors took turns caring for them.

Hoy stopped in daily to check on his wife, but could not stay long; he had to keep working to provide for his family of seven. Before he married Sylvia, Hoy worked at the Jewell Milk Company. Then, in 1925, he was deputy sheriff for a while. He found his niche when he was put in charge of the Pitkin's Provision's meat department, which would lead him to opening his own business in the future. Sylvia's recovery took a long time, but she eventually regained her strength. She returned home and soon was well enough to care for all of the five children. Baby Paul was held in his mother's arms, at home, for the first time.

As Paul grew up, he thought his parents' names were quite comical. His dad answered the phone, "Hoy Lynde," and people thought he was Chinese. His mother's name was Sylvia Bell, and there were plenty of jokes about Tinkerbelle. Paul would later create Hoysly Productions which he named in honor of his parents. His parents often took him and his siblings to Olentangy Park, in Columbus. His Mom packed up lots of great picnic food, and after the feast they would all go to The Columbus Zoo. Picnics became one of Paul's favorite pastimes throughout his life.

In 1928, Paul's father was elected sheriff of Knox County. Paul told everyone, "I grew up in a prison," and he literally did — for four years. Part of the benefit of being the sheriff included housing. Hoy, Sylvia, and all five of their children, moved into the apartment attached to the jailhouse. Paul's father was well respected in Knox County, and it was usually a safe place; however, Hoy was sheriff during the time of Prohibition. "This made the job very dangerous," Nancy explained about her grandfather. "Grandpa Lynde had to go out on calls to take the illegal stills down. He would round up his deputies and go after the people making liquor. Many nights, no one knew if Grandpa would make it home."

That same year, Paul's mother gave birth to her sixth and last child, Johnny. This time it was almost too much for her body to bear. She was near death. She was rushed again to Mercy Hospital, which was located right next door to the jail. Hoy was beside himself, and Paul was once again without his mother.

The nuns were happy to see Paul and gladly took him back into their care. This time they took in the new baby too. The nuns and nurses took turns holding and cooing over the new Lynde arrival. Paul wanted his mother, and he could not go to her. On top of that, Johnny was stealing his spotlight. He was so jealous of his baby brother that he told Jane Wilkie of *TV Guide* that he tried to put him in a basket with the hopes that if he shuffled him around with the other infants, the nurses would not be able to figure out who he belonged to. "This was a very hard time for Johnny and Paul and all the Lynde family," Nancy said.

The toddler soon found something to look forward to three times a day: the meals at the hospital. Paul just loved eating with the nuns. Food was bringing some comfort, along with the way the nuns fussed over him. These surrogate mothers took little Paul with them all over the hospital as they made their rounds. The nurses spoiled him too and allowed him to have the run of the place. The nuns took turns telling him bedtime stories each night. As he grew older, they even taught him to read.

When Paul was able to return home, he would sneak next door again, back over to the hospital. When he turned five, the nuns took him to see his first movie: *Ben Hur.* According to its trailer, the silent film had a cast of 150,000. Young Paul watched wide-eyed as Ramon Novarro rode his chariot and commanded his white horses with their thundering hoofs to race faster. He was mesmerized by the powerful roman officer, played by Francis X. Bushman, and he sat with his mouth open during the epic sea battle. When the picture ended, he was determined to one day be an actor, for that was a sure way to become rich and also famous.

After a very long recovery, Sylvia was released from the hospital. She returned to the things she loved: her husband, her children, and cooking. Sylvia was an excellent cook, and the table talk revolved around food as they ate their meal. "At breakfast we discussed what we were having for lunch; at lunch we discussed what we were having for dinner," an adult Paul told Jacquelyn Nicholson, of *Bon Appetit* magazine.

Paul continued his love affair with food. After lunch, he would go out to play with the kids from the neighborhood. Sometimes he spotted a hot pie cooling on someone's window sill, and he would grab it and run. He would then hide out while he ate the evidence. He was growing wider faster than he was growing taller. The nine-year-old was a bit chubby, and as he walked to Elmwood Elementary School, he was sometimes made fun of. One kid used to taunt him by taking his hat and playing keep away with it. He was shy and had a hard time defending himself.

When Paul was ten years old, his appendix burst and he became gravely ill. The doctors at the hospital were concerned about operating because their young patient was overweight.

Paul had peritonitis — an inflammation in the wall of the abdomen — which, during the 1930s, usually resulted in death. Gangrene had also set in. The doctors hooked the ten-year-old up to an I.V., which dripped saline solution into his veins. It would be the only source of food he would be permitted to have for a while. It was another trying time for the Lynde family. His parents took turns going to the hospital to sit with their critically ill son day after day, month after month. The nuns were there too. When the doctors saw their patient was getting well, they put him on solid food, but instructed him not to overeat as they wanted him to lose weight. Paul knew so many of the staff there that he always charmed someone into getting him more food. After seven long months, Paul was allowed to go home, but with orders to stay in bed. Hoy then went into his son's room and carried his bed into the dining room, next to the kitchen. Sylvia spent much of her day at the stove, so here she had a perfect view of the patient. Sylvia used lots of starch in her meals to feed her family of eight; this was during the Depression, and starch was cheap. Every time she left the kitchen, she would bring her son a plate of biscuits and gravy, and potatoes. She often joined Paul for the meals, sitting beside him as they ate. Once again, Paul found comfort in food.

Sylvia was happy to see her son eating and getting well. When the time came to remove his bandages, Paul gasped at the new design he had on his body. "My incision looked like the surgeon tore my appendix out with his hands," he said. After nearly a year of being bedridden, the young boy was ready to get out of bed. He forced his legs over the side, and when he attempted to stand, his legs couldn't endure the weight. He had gained one hundred pounds. "I had to learn to walk again." Paul said. When his legs built up some strength, he was finally able to go outside. Some of the kids in the neighborhood began to make fun of his size. The quiet kid went back inside.

It was time for the fifth grader to return to school. Sylvia had a hard time finding pants that would fit her son, who now weighed more than her husband. His mother saw how much his size bothered him. She looked at his sad green eyes and said, "You hold it well."

As Paul walked to school, a few kids started to call him names, but Paul said something that cracked them up. He was relieved they were laughing with him, not at him. When he entered the classroom, he was packing an orginal wit, one that would boomerang and ricochet around the classroom. His fellow students found him to be the funniest kid in the school. Many were magnetized by the big kid's personality. The school photographer captured his effects when he snapped the class photo: The boy standing next to Paul, who was half his size, in both weight and height, put his arm around his pal as they posed for the picture. "I made them laugh to distract them from my being fat. I was never called 'Tubby' or 'Lard Ass' like other overweight kids." Paul said, "I was grateful for that."

Gym class was brutal for the overweight kid who had been immobile for the past year. The boys at school were kept in shape, as it was a time of war and Paul was battling his own. "I looked like Kate Smith's niece," he said. The gym teacher blew the whistle signaling the class to start their calisthenics; Paul prayed his shorts would not split. Paul noticed some of his classmates were excused from gym to go to band practice, so he told his teacher he wanted to play an instrument. He was relieved he no longer had to go to gym class, but had a problem with the band's school uniform; he couldn't close the jacket and it was the largest one there. He then decided he would play the bass drum; it was so big it went over the front of his uniform and no one knew it wasn't able to button.

On Saturdays, Paul headed to the movie theater in town, with huge bags of popcorn that his mother had made. He was still in awe of the actors, and the big screen still captivated him. After the show, he would wander around the neighborhood looking for just the kind of house he pictured a movie star would live in.

According to Connie Rice, Paul's youngest niece, there was a mansion in town that stood out from all the other homes, and Paul used to fantasize that he would live in it one day when he became rich. He used to sit on the steps of that house and wave at the cars passing by, to make it look like he lived there. He told a reporter, "I guess I fought back having delusions of grandeur." Those delusions, along with his passion and determination, would allow him to buy that house one day if he wanted to, or an even bigger one.

When Paul was eleven years old, his father opened Lynde's East Side Market. At first he liked the idea of his father owning his own business and he got a charge out of seeing his last name on the sign. What he didn't like was that his dad was a butcher; he didn't like the image it could conjure up. The next time someone asked him what his father did for a living, he would say, "He's a cattle surgeon." Most everyone in town shopped at the store. It had great cuts of meats and the atmosphere was friendly. Hoy often had his two oldest male children, Richard and Cordy, help him out. Paul and Johnny would be recruited a few years later. The four boys didn't mind when they had to help behind the counter or package the meat. It was the mid-week rush that they dreaded. That's when they had to actually become butchers. "They just hated it," Nancy said. "They had to kill chickens on Thursday and clean them and dress them so they would be ready for the customers' Sunday dinners. Paul's classmates would make squawking noises when they saw him, and they called him "Chicken Plucker."

As Paul got a little older, his father let him work behind the counter, alongside of him, to help sell the meat. His shy demeanor along with his irresistible grin seemed to get the customers to open their purses a little wider. Hoy told him he outshined his brothers when it came to selling. This was a huge compliment, coming from his father. For the first time, Paul felt a sense of pride. It was the only thing he felt he was good at. "Basically an actor is salesman," he summarized years later. He thought his three brothers were all better than he was. He described them as "Richard the athlete, Cordy the brain, Johnny the baby, and Paul the nothing."

Paul's favorite brother was Cordy. His parents, too, favored him over all their children, but Paul never seemed bitter about that. "He was my mother's favorite and deserved to be," he said. Cordy was choir president, president of the French Club, carnival manager, and in drama club. He also edited the high school yearbook. Paul had the same teachers as his brother had in school, and they had high expectations for him, but Paul preferred clowning around to studying. The teachers called Cordy "The brain," and they referred to Paul as "The silly goose."

After Cordy graduated, he enlisted in overseas action. No one was aware of it then, but Cordy was about to fight in what would be one of the largest and bloodiest battles fought in World War II: The Battle of the Bulge.

While Cordy was off at war, Paul's niece Nancy recalled the Lynde family visiting them at their home in nearby Danville, Ohio. Though Paul was her uncle, he was only eleven years older than her. "Johnny was close to Paul's age and they ran together. They would pick me up in the car and Paul would be driving and the two of them would just tease me to no end," Nancy said. At the end of the afternoon, the cousins would head back to join the rest of the relatives for dinner. Paul's sister Grace and his mom would prepare the meal. Nancy remembers Paul's mom as sweet. "Grandma Sylvia had a big heart, as big as the outdoors. Grandpa Hoy had a great sense of humor."

Hoy and Sylvia had a strong marriage. Nancy said, "Grandma and Grandpa were very much in love right up until they died." According to Paul, his dad worshipped his mom. Finding that kind of love would become one of his life's quests.

"Paul and his Siblings" FRONT: Richard, Cordy, Paul & Helen. BACK: Grace.
COURTESY OF CONNIE RICE AND NANCY NOCE

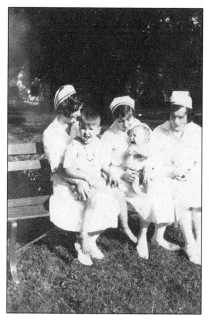

LEFT: Paul and his baby brother, Johnny, and the nurses who took care of them at Mercy Hospital. COURTESY OF CONNIE RICE AND NANCY NOCE
RIGHT: "I looked like Kate Smith's niece." Young Paul as a boy scout.

Paul performing at Northwestern. COURTESY OF NORTHWESTERN UNIVERSITY ARCHIVES

CHAPTER 2

Lynde's First Loves

"Can you see me as a football player?...
Now that's acting." PAUL LYNDE

Paul had met Marilyn Surlas when he was in the eighth grade, and according to Marilyn, he fell in love with her after she had given him a maple sugarman confection to eat. They dated on and off through junior high and high school. "Paul had a great sense of humor," she recalled. He enjoyed her similar sense of humor as well, and they were always making each other laugh. Marilyn was Protestant and belonged to an Episcopal church, which she attended regularly with her family. According to Marilyn, though Paul was Methodist, he switched religions because of her. When he was asked the name of his new church, he said, "It's called St. Paul's, named after me."

The young man was quite shy and more serious when he was alone with his girl, but did not appear that way when he was surrounded by their friends. He amused the gang with his wicked wit at Hecklers Drug Store, where they went after school for shakes and soda.

"Paul was funny, smart, and wonderful," Marilyn said. From the age of fourteen and right through high school, Paul thought they would marry. Marilyn was not as serious as her boyfriend was about their relationship. Later, Paul told the *Sarasota Herald Tribune* that he blamed his weight. "It was the ridiculous way I looked," he said. For Paul though, she would be the one he would refer to all his life as the one he wanted to marry. "She was an obsession," he said.

Paul never forgot his first love: acting. And in 1942, he took part in Mount Vernon High School's production of *Mr. and Mrs. North*. He played Buano, and he truly loved being on stage. It was under those lights that he felt noticed, not for his size but for his talent. By his senior year, Paul had become quite popular and continued acting in school plays, which were directed by Ruth Druxall. She saw promise in his acting ability and had several discussions with her student about his desire to continue acting after high school. She encouraged him to consider attending Northwestern University, in Evanston, Illinois, where she had attended.

As the school year came to a close, the senior made up his mind to follow her advice and pursue his dreams. He would, however, have to tell his father, who did not think acting was a real career. "I was afraid of my father, but I could get anything I wanted to from my mother," Paul said. His dad couldn't understand his son's passion for acting and he tried to talk sense into him about a real future, like taking over his store one day. Paul pleaded with his mom; he just had to go to Northwestern University. It was the best drama school in the country. When Sylvia realized just how serious her son was about this, she talked her husband into paying for his college tuition.

In the fall of 1944, Paul stepped on the same campus that Academy Award-winners Charlton Heston and Patricia Neal were walking on. Charlton Heston was there on a drama scholarship and would later win two Academy Awards, including one for Best Actor in a Leading Role in *Ben-Hur*. Patricia Neal was a sophomore and had just been crowned syllabus queen in Northwestern's all-campus beauty pageant. She would go on to win many awards, including an Oscar, for her role in *Hud*, just ten years after she left Northwestern. Paul was just as determined to make his mark in the acting world as Charleston and Patricia were.

The freshman still enjoyed singing, and he sang in Northwestern's a cappella choir. He also took a course in "Introduction to Oral Interpretation." The first assignment was for the students to write a speech and recite it for the class. Paul went back to his room and feverishly wrote a lengthy monologue about a subject no other student would dare to discuss. When it was his turn to speak the next day, he began by addressing the class as if he was the health inspector for the school. His topic: sexual relations. "Point number one: sexual troubles begin in the home…," he announced. His professor, Dr. Lee, stood there listening with her mouth wide open, but moments later, she joined the rest of the students, who were falling off their chairs, laughing. When the class was dismissed, the students burst through the classroom doors and ran to tell their friends of the hilarious guy they just heard. By the next day, just about every student on campus knew his name.

Though Paul's speech was quite comical, he was really looking forward to his drama class to do some serious acting. When he was asked to recite from *Macbeth*, he opened his mouth, but before he could finish the line, the class was screaming with laughter. Paul continued, but the laughter only increased. Somehow the sight of this 260-pound young man with his campy, nasally, thick Ohioan accent reading Shakespeare just made the students howl. The director, Claudia Webster, had to stop her student in order to keep the class under control. She told him he would have to read for her in her office. She just looked at him and said, "You'll be perfect as the lead, in the *Male Animal.*" Paul was such a hit as Wally, the football player, and he later said, "Can you see me as a football player?... Now *that's* acting!"

At Northwestern, Paul hung out with three special classmates who would become his lifelong friends. The first one he met was Jan Steinkirshner, who later married and became Jan Forbes. According to Jan, she had first met Paul on campus after a student had approached her and asked her if her last name was Lynde. She said no. "Well there's a guy here who looks and talks just like you," the student told her.

About a week later, this roly-poly fellow came up to Jan and said, "Oh, so you're the one." It was Paul. "We both had big teeth and watery green eyes. We became fast friends," Jan said. He called her his Tiny Twin. "He used to sit in our early morning speech class and say to me in *that* voice, 'I'm going to be rich and f-a-a-a-mous.'" The two wrote to each other after college, and even decades later, Paul began each letter to her with: Dear Tiny.

The freshman headed to his drama class where the seats were arranged in alphabetical order. Paul's seat was next to a young lady named Charlotte Lubotsky. Charlotte had been singing since she was a child and had hopes of becoming a serious actress. They struck up a conversation and a friendship began.

Paul then wrote skits, which he and Charlotte would act out. She later changed her last name and became known as Charlotte Rae. She would make her Broadway debut in 1952, in *Three Wishes for Jamie,* and she would become a regular on *Car 54, Where Are You?* She was nominated for two Emmys, including one for her dramatic role in *Queen of the Stardust Ballroom,* and also made many television appearances. She is probably best remembered for her role as Mrs. Garret, the housemother, in the television show *The Facts of Life.*

Jan was in her sophomore year when she met her roommate, who would become a lifelong friend to the trio. Her name was Cloris Leachman. Jan introduced Cloris to Charlotte and Paul; instantly there was chemistry between them. The hopeful actors created harmony at the campus piano, where they made up silly songs and laughed as they sang them. The other students were so entertained watching them and couldn't wait to see what they were working on next. Cloris and Paul were in a play, The *Doctor in Spite of Himself*. "I had a small part and Paul had the lead and he was just hysterical," Cloris said. As their friendship grew, so did their acting skills. Years later, Cloris would win an Academy Award for Best Supporting Actress in the *Last Picture Show* and eight prime-time Emmys. She played Phyllis in *The Mary Tyler Moore Show* and starred in a spin-off from that show: *Phyllis*. In Mel Brooks's *Young Frankenstein*, she played Frau Blücher, and she acted in many other significant films. Cloris is still acting today and can be seen on the sitcom *Raising Hope*.

During those years at college, Paul wrote many letters to his high school girlfriend. According to Marilyn, some of his letters were hilarious. She had a shoebox filled with them. He would also write sweet letters and ask her to visit him, but Marilyn never did. He stayed loyal to her and did not date anyone throughout college.

Paul joined a fraternity, Phi Kappa Sigma, and he would often perform for his brothers. According to authors Joe Florenski and Steve Wilson of *Center Square*, he played a large Scarlet O'Hara in a satire of *Gone with the Wind*. In one scene, Paul was gobbling down a smorgasbord of eats of all sorts and declared, "As God is my witness; I'll never be hungry again."

For a short time, Paul worked on the weekends at the Toddle House, a diner-style restaurant in Evansville. Cloris and Jan came by often. "He used to serve us the greatest potatoes and give us food for free," Cloris recalled. Paul was so popular that herds of his fellow students would come in to eat during his shift. The restaurant had an honor system: Paul was supposed to drop the check in a box for each table that he served, but no matter what his friends and fellow students ordered, he only charged everyone seven cents. He wondered how the establishment never figured out why they made the least amount of money when it was the most crowded.

Back on campus, Paul continued socializing and entertaining. His humor was becoming more biting, which he referred to as sadistic satire, and the students loved it. He appreciated their admiration so much that he began skipping classes, just to entertain them.

Paul and Charlotte won roles in the annual Women's Athletic Association and the Men's Union, known as Waa-Mu. In these off-campus productions, Northwestern students write, perform, and present a musical. Paul helped write some of the skits and lyrics for the show.

He and Charlotte ruled the stage during their years together there and were considered Waa-Mu's favorites. Both were there to become serious actors, and when the two of them were on stage together, there was never a dry eye in the house — from laughing. Charlotte would say her lines in a way that made those in the auditorium explode with laughter. Then, a very large Paul would speak, adding twisted, comical faces. He had an almost vicious type of humor that, once caught on, caused another outbreak of hysteria. They were so famous on campus that they became known as "Lubotsky and Lynde." They were regularly interviewed for the campus newspaper, *Daily Northwestern*, by Glenn Church, and one time Charlotte told the paper that when audiences grew to understand Paul's humor, he would become famous. Paul told the same reporter that Charlotte illuminated the stage and added, "It's hell to play with Char, I keep thinking I'm getting the laugh only to find out that Char moved an eyelash."

Though they were just good friends, some of the students thought they would make a good couple. In those days, if a guy wanted to make a certain girl his official girlfriend, he would pin her. One section of the school's paper, called "Kampus Keyhole," wrote that neither Paul nor Charlotte was pinned, but that they should be by the way they carried on together.

During one theatre production, Paul and Charlotte were performing on stage where the scene required the two to toast their glasses. Somehow, Charlotte hit Paul's mouth with the glass and it chipped his tooth. Paul went on performing, but said it was hard for him to say his lines with the damaged done to his mouth.

According to Kevin B. Leonard, the Archivist at Northwestern, based on his close reviews of many available records, Paul Lynde was unquestionably among the most very talented, visible, hard-working, and admired Northwestern students of his era. His accomplishments, especially in theatrical productions and in the University's Waa-Mu Show — in acting, writing, singing, staging, and organizing — were widely and eagerly anticipated, notable, polished, hilarious, reviewed, praised, and admired. With his fellow student Charlotte (Lubotsky) Rae, Lynde dominated Northwestern's performing arts community with his talent, humor, energy, and drive.

In his last year, Paul became President of the Senior Council and spoke to the seniors about their responsibilities after graduation. He said hard work and luck would be a key factor in making it as a professional actor. Paul was feeling on top of the world during his college days; then his world fell apart. His parents received the dreaded news that their son,

Cordy, had been lost in the war. Paul was scared; he might never see his brother again. Hoy tried to be strong for Sylvia, who feared so much for her son that her health took a turn for the worse.

A few months later, Paul was due to graduate. It was the night before graduation, and he was just made aware that he had failed what he thought was the easiest course Northwestern offered. He joked it was something simple like, "sock folding," which he rarely showed up for. He didn't understand what the grade "V" meant. He asked his professor what it stood for. He replied, "visitor." When his father, who was quite frank, called on the phone and said, 'What the hell is V for?' He didn't believe his son for a second when he rattled off, "Valedictorian."

Paul was informed he was not graduating. His mom was too ill to travel, but his dad was already in the car on his way. Paul panicked. He ran all over town the night before and again that morning, trying to find the proper authority who could save him. He finally spoke to the Student Senate who held a meeting. "So while the orchestra was playing, I was handed my cap and gown," Paul said. "The ink was still wet on my diploma when they handed it to me, and my dad never knew."

The relieved graduate departed Northwestern with the best actor award under his arm and headed for Broadway. He was quite confident that he would become a star overnight. His delusions of grandeur were about to be shattered. The city would attempt to devour him and test his soul just to see how determined he really was to become rich and famous.

Paul's High School Graduation, Mt. Vernon, Ohio (1944).
PHOTO COURTESY OF NANCY NOCE AND CONNIE RICE

"Lubotsky and Lynde." Charlotte Rae and Paul (in back) performing a Waa-Mu
Production. COURTESY OF NORTHWESTERN UNIVERSITY ARCHIVES

CHAPTER 3

Food for Blood

"I became the playboy of New York." PAUL LYNDE

New York was the first Hollywood, with its glamorous night clubs and spotlights that scanned the stars above and below Broadway. It was a tough town for actors, but it was one of the few places that offered open cast calls. You didn't need an agent to audition, but you sure needed guts, determination, and, above all, talent that could surpass the city's already finest talent.

When Paul arrived in New York, he looked up the names he was given by an actress he met; born Catherine Gloria Balotta from Cleveland Ohio, she changed her name and was known as Kaye Ballard. Though she was only a year older than Paul, she had already performed on Broadway. Paul couldn't get over this. Kaye had been performing in Chicago doing *Three to Make Ready* at the Blackstone Theater. The singer and actress would go on to perform in many Broadway plays, movies, television shows, and also became a regular on *The Doris Day Show*. She would become best known, by many, for her role in the television sitcom *The Mothers-in-Law*.

Kaye first noticed Paul when she had gone to see a Northwestern, Waa-Mu production, which had traveled to the windy city with their cast. Charlotte and Paul were in that show and Kaye, who had an eye for talent, was amazed with how professional it was. She thought Paul was so hilarious. "That guy is truly going to be a star," she said. She was so impressed with him that she called Broadway producer Leonard Sillman, telling him he just had to see this guy. She chatted with Paul after the show and gave him some names to contact when he arrived in New York.

With his new friend's connections, Paul was hanging out with all the right people shortly after he arrived in the big city. He met directors, producers, playwrights, and attended cast parties. He seemed more interested in being around actors than focusing on becoming one himself. He seemed to forget why he was there. "For the first few years I became the playboy of New York," he said.

He lived recklessly off the money his father sent him, using it to support his partying lifestyle. He loved mingling with all the theater folk and would entertain everyone with his way-out humor at those cast parties. Afterwards, Paul would dive deeper into the night life, finding the after-hour's clubs, which he did not leave until the sun came up. He couldn't get enough of New York. The city and the people made him feel so alive. He would never forget the feeling it gave him, and he later would choose that city to spend the second half of his life in. He would buy a brownstone there, but never get the chance to live in it.

Cloris had already been living in New York for a while and was studying at the Actors Studio. She had left Northwestern before Paul because she won $1,000 for coming in third place in a Miss America Pageant. She had her debut on Broadway with Katherine Hepburn in *As You Like It*. Charlotte had also arrived, and she was performing in theaters and nightclubs throughout the city. Occasionally, the two girls would meet with 'Paulie,' as they called him, and Jan would travel from Pennsylvania to New York to be with them. After Jan had left Northwestern, she got married and began having children. She was no longer interested in a career, but always kept in touch with her three buddies.

Paul knew he was lagging behind his college classmates, Cloris and Charlotte. His excuse was that he did not have an agent and he couldn't afford to hire a writer. Part of him feared he wouldn't have the luck that was needed to make it in this business. Part of him still clung to his belief that he was born to be famous.

Paul was living in a building across from Carnegie Hall that he shared with other residents, including Marlon Brando, Wally Cox, and Steve Cochrane. Each floor had a bathroom and a kitchen for the tenants to share. The refrigerators were kept out in the halls. When everyone was asleep, Paul would go from floor to floor, sneaking food from each refrigerator. One late night, he crept out of bed and went down the hall where he quietly opened the fridge door. He was shocked to find a note that read:

PAUL LYNDE, FOR YOUR INFORMATION, ONE OF THESE BOWLS CONTAINS POISON. TAKE YOUR CHOICE.

He wondered who left the note, since most of the tenants were also starving actors, and he presumed they were stealing food like he was.

Paul continued stepping out each evening to parties hosted by his actor friends. His foot-long grin, followed by his infectious maniacal laugh, had a few people in the industry interested. Paul was inching himself into the spotlight, but then he was cast back into the shadows. He had just received word that his brother's body had been found.

This was in the beginning of February 1949, when the Army notified the Lynde family of the news. According to Paul's niece Nancy, those years were very strenuous on Paul and his family. Paul's brother Cordy had been missing in action since 1940, and now, nine years later, Cordy was pronounced dead. All hopes of his return vanished. A few weeks later, on February 23, Paul's mother died of a heart attack. "The news actually killed her," Paul told a reporter, "She died from a broken heart." He headed home to bury his mother. He had loved her very much and would miss her sweetness and warmth.

Paul returned to New York with a heavy heart. Three months later, Cordy's remains arrived in Mount Vernon for a military burial. Once again, Paul headed back to his hometown, this time to attend his brother's burial. Paul stood there with his newly widowed father, who was watching his second-born being buried. The very next day Hoy had a massive heart attack. He was only fifty-four years old. Paul had another family member to bury.

"My parents were young and very much in love, they simply died of broken hearts over a son who was their favorite of the six of us," Paul later said in an interview. With three family members dead in just a matter of months, Paul headed back to New York shielded in shock.

Not long after that, the twenty-three-year-old received a piece of mail from his hometown. As he opened the envelope and began reading, his fragmented heart splintered again. It was a wedding announcement — Marilyn was getting married and he was invited to the reception.

The bride and groom held a private ceremony with just family and a few friends, followed by a large reception at the country club in Mount Vernon. Paul arrived alone. According to Marilyn, when he saw her friend, he asked her how the ceremony went. She said, "Just fine."

"Perfect," Paul said sarcastically, "just the way the divorce will go." Paul stayed for the party and, later, told a reporter that he went home afterwards and sobbed uncontrollably.

Paul returned to New York, his fantasies of marriage to Marilyn evaporated. He was so broke he didn't even have enough money to meet his friends for drinks. He had to do something to survive. He would have to get a job. No money would be sent to him ever again. He later admitted that his father's death forced him to do something about his career. Paul worked as a hotel clerk for a short while, then at Atkins Department Store, and later, his favorite job, as a waiter. When those jobs ended, he went to work as an ambulance driver, where part of the perk was an apartment to live in rent free. After he moved in, he was told he was on call twenty-four hours a day, so he could never leave the place.

It wasn't so bad at first. He drove elderly people to rest homes or sometimes hospitals, but he wasn't prepared to pick up his next passenger. He received a call to pick up a patient one afternoon. Paul arrived at the man's home and knocked on the door, but there was no answer. He called out, went inside, and saw the elderly gentlemen sitting in his chair. Paul went over to him and then realized he was dead. Paul ran out of there; he had seen enough of death. As he passed by the ambulance he had parked, he put his cap on the front seat and never went back.

Paul did not have enough money to buy food and he was tired of being hungry. Out of desperation, he sold his blood. The going price was five dollars for a pint of blood; Paul said it felt like five hundred dollars to him. He returned every six weeks, and said he would have gone more frequently, but that was the minimum amount of time permitted to give more blood. He waited anxiously on the long lines. He couldn't believe he had to do this. He was supposed to be rich and famous by now. Cloris and Charlotte were well on their way. He shouldn't be in this position. As he waited in line, he recognized several despaired faces from the last time he was there. An alcoholic in front of him, who reeked of liquor, was next to give his blood, but was refused. Paul watched the pathetic man crumble. "He got down on his knees and begged and cried," Paul said. He vowed he would never forget that scene, "But you do," he admitted.

Paul gave his blood, rested a bit, and left. His head hung low as his feet pounded the pavement. For one flickering moment he thought about throwing his dream away: he would settle for becoming a teacher. Then he saw a nearly six-foot-tall man in a reflection of a store window. At first, he only saw the chubby face and a large belly. Then he remembered what his mom used to say to him when he was a young boy, "You hold it well."

The determination he felt a while back returned to him. He smiled with his titanic teeth and thought, "I *am* going to be rich and famous." He wanted a drink and some food, and so he headed towards the village. He looked at the only money he had: the five dollars blood money that was clutched in his hand. He thought of one of the lines he recited in college, when he played the role as Scarlet O'Hara: "As God is my witness, I will never go hungry again." And he wouldn't.

TOP: Coradon Lynde, Paul's brother. LEFT: Paul's father, Hoy Coradon Lynde. RIGHT: Paul's mother, Sylvia Bell Doup Lynde.

Paul with his two basset hounds, Orville and Wilbur. COURTESY OF CONNIE RICE AND NANCY NOCE

CHAPTER 4

Beyond Therapy

"That's one woman I could have married." PAUL LYNDE

A 250-pound Paul walked alone on the crowded streets in Greenwich Village. It was the day before Thanksgiving, and the city was swarming with tourists arriving to see the premiere of *Guys and Dolls*. He ached to be in a Broadway show like that. He couldn't figure out why he wasn't getting any call backs from the auditions he had gone on.

It had been two years since he walked out of Northwestern University with the best actor of the year award, and Paul couldn't believe he wasn't a big star yet. He thought that by now he would have had some real recognition. This was New York; he just couldn't understand what was taking so long.

Paul was tired of living in a dump and being broke. He felt ashamed that he had conned his father into sending him money to help him with his "career," but had used it all on excess eating and drinking. There would be no more money coming in. Those days were gone. So were his father, mother, and his favorite brother. The three of them abandoned him, almost all at once. Paul wasn't giving up; he knew he was meant to be rich and famous.

He arrived at One Fifth Avenue, a supper club he frequented, and got himself a drink. Someone at the club suggested Paul enter their amateur contest, which they were having the following night. When he saw the prize money, he immediately ran back to his apartment and, in a frenzy, wrote an outlandish, dark, humorous monologue he called "My Four Swell Days in Africa with the Trip of the Month Club." After a sleepless night, Paul returned to the club and grabbed a drink, hoping it would help calm his acute anxiety. Then he stepped on the stage to become Carl Canker, appearing before the audience with his head wrapped in bandages, with his arm in a sling, and leaning on a crutch. In his nasal Midwestern twang and sarcastic tone, he recounted his safari adventure, in which he got gored by a rhinoceros, went over a waterfall, and his wife got eaten by a lion...yet he was determined to finish the tour:

> We had been tramping on the trail about four or five hours, when my wife complained of her feet. The only shoes she had were those high-heeled sling pumps, she just couldn't take it. So we had to leave her there out on the trail. A couple days later on the way back, I found this piece of her dress along with her purse and gloves and to this day, I don't know what happened to her [lets out a large, cynical Lynde laugh] but what I really remember about that day was, it was the only day it didn't rain, and I got to take some dandy snapshots...

The audience and judges loved this twenty-four-year-old comedian's unique style and sardonic humor about a man who laughs his way through tragedies. Paul won the contest! He was handed the prize money and was offered one week's engagement. After some celebrating, he left. And, just like Carl Canker but without visible wounds, he too was determined to finish the tour.

That performance awarded him two more gigs at top entertainment clubs. This was the chance he had been waiting for. Now he would show New York his talent. He practiced his monologue over and over on the way to his new gig. He arrived at the very posh Versailles Supper Club on 151 East 50th Street, one of the finest restaurant-cabarets in the world. He nervously stepped on the stage, and in a matter of moments, he realized that no amount of practice could have prepared him for this crowd.

"I played sixteen weeks, two shows a night, and I would bomb every performance," Paul told the host of *The Tonight Show* about his first experiences doing standup comedy. He begged the owner of the club to fire him, but he wouldn't. Paul was doing his African monologue when, all of a sudden, the audience got up in the middle of his act and started dancing. "And there's no music in my a-a-a-a-a-ct."

Paul wasn't so sure anymore if he wanted to continue this type of work. He found the past few weeks to be grueling, but he was booked for another performance that April, at Spivey's Rooftop on 57th Street and Lexington. The club was on the top floor in a penthouse. It had opened in 1940, and was owned by Spivey LeVoe. She had become successful singing and playing piano in cabarets and speakeasies before she opened her own place. Described as a large and handsome woman by one reporter, Spivey had a way of making songs sound quite risqué, as she did when singing, "I Didn't Do A Thing Last Night." Some of her supporting acts in the past had been Liberace and Carol Channing. She charged a three dollar entrance fee on weekends, and although her place seated 100, she packed in closer to 300 on some nights, when she had first opened her doors.

Paul gave a short nod to the elevator man as he stepped inside with his crutch and rolls of bandages. They rode to the ninth floor, where Paul got off and found Spivey. He waited for the crowd to show up, but Spivey told him not to expect too much because business had been lousy lately. A while later, they heard the sound of the elevator moving and Spivey shouted, "Get your props. You're on!" Paul scrambled in vain, as it was only the elevator man, who just wanted someone to talk to. The next time the elevator doors opened, it was the landlord trying to hunt Spivey down for the rent money.

The weekends sprouted some customers, and Paul did his African safari adventure for them. When he finished his act, he told the audience Spivey would now perform for them, but then she would disappear. "Most nights she would lock herself in the john," Paul said. He couldn't understand it because after she closed the club, she would let Judy Garland, Martha Raye, and Judy Holiday come in, and she would sing for them. Paul was not aware of it, but years later Spivey told the press she often experienced stage fright with nightclub audiences. Paul was just grateful to be getting a paycheck each week. One day, he was heading to work and was suddenly stopped in his tracks, "I arrived at the club and saw the piano under the canopy on the sidewalk and knew it was over."

Paul left empty handed and watched the bright lights of his beloved city fade. He went to his new apartment on the east side of Manhattan and waited by the phone for more offers, but the phone never rang. New York was failing him, and he was forced to leave town. He packed a bag and left for summer stock in Corning, New York. His first paying job as an actor was at the Corning Summer Theater, playing Pon in *Happy Birthday*. Paul would go over and over his lines beforehand, but still had his bout with stage fright. He was consumed with fear, but once he stepped onto the stage, he appeared perfectly composed.

Paul finally felt someone had noticed his talent, when he was cast as one of the leads in *Anything Goes*, as Billy Crocker. Next, he played the role of the district attorney in *Dream Girls*, with Judy Holiday. Now he was bumping elbows and touring with some real names. Paul was becoming very fond of the theater life, and the audiences enjoyed him. He was disappointed after that production when he was only given a small part in *Showboat*, and again just a supporting player as Steve, in *A Streetcar Named Desire*. Paul was filling up his resumé, but not with many lead roles. He realized that part of the reason was his weight, so he began to eat less and dropped a few pounds.

In 1952, Leonard Sillman was putting together another revue of *New Faces*. The first one was in 1934, and each show would also consist of new talents: singing, dancing, and comedy skits. This was where so many greats like Henry Fonda, Van Johnson, and Imogene Coca were first discovered. Paul just had to be in that show. He called Mr. Sillman, and he auditioned right over the phone for him with his African monologue. He made the cut.

After unending hours of practice and hard work by the new talent, the anticipated opening night arrived on May 16. Paul waited backstage with sixteen other excited and nervous new faces. Among them were Eartha Kitt, Alice Ghostley, Virginia De Luce, Robert Clary, Jimmy Russell, Virginia Bosler, along with Leonard Sillmans's sister, June Carroll. Each one hoping this would be their big break.

Outside, shiny white Rolls Royces and other swanky cars pulled up to the Royal Theatre on 45th Street. The show would attract big stars such as Ethel Merman, Greta Garbo, and Rex Harrison, along with politicians and some royalty, who would be seen sitting in the best seats in the house. Dressed to the nines, tourists and New Yorkers mobbed the buzzing lobby as they gave in their ticket and were handed the playbill. There, the names of the new talents were typed below the smaller print warnings: not to light matches during the show and to obey the management in the event of an air raid alarm. Ads of Bellows whiskey and Philip Morris cigarettes followed. Ladies were reminded to remove their hats.

Paul paced backstage, reading his lines in the crowded dressing area. He lit another cigarette as he rehearsed. His anxiety was mounting as his thoughts taunted him. He was afraid he would forget his lines. What if no one laughed? Then someone announced, "Places everybody." Some of the cast members were chatting about how many movie stars and important people were in the audience that night. Paul's eyes bulged with fear, his anxiety climbed; he couldn't listen anymore and had to remove himself. His costars looked baffled. He walked away with increased mental strain. If he found out that anyone famous would be watching, it would cripple him.

When Paul heard his cue, he hobbled on stage with his crutch, his head wrapped in bandages, and his arm in a sling. He began by explaining how he won the trip of the month, and then he told the bizarre story, "There are several approaches to the jungle," he said in a shaky, nasally voice. "My wife and I found them all, being dropped from an airplane was our favorite." He delivered his "Trip of the Month Club" — the African Safari Monologue — with what would become his signature sardonic delivery. He got through it with perfection, and the audience loved him.

Paul realized he may not be the main attraction in this show, the way he had been at Northwestern. He couldn't get over how much talent was in one room. He hoped he would stand out. Paul also performed in a few other skits, including one called "Of Father and Sons," with Alice Ghostley, Ronny Graham, Allen Conway, and Jimmy Russell, written by Mel Brooks.

Jimmy Russell, Ronny Graham, and Paul were in a skit together called "Crazy Man," which Ronny also helped write. Ronny solely wrote the lyrics and music for "Lucky Pierre." Pierre was played by Robert Clary, who later became well known from his role as Corporal LeBeau, the French prisoner, in *Hogan's Heroes*. According to Robert, the whole cast got along well. Previews were fair, but opening night was the complete opposite. Alice Ghostley stopped the show with *Boston Beguine* in the first act, Robert stopped the show with *I'm In Love With Miss Logan*, and in the second act, Eartha Kitt did the same, with *Monotonous*. They stopped the show every single time seven days a week. They were a big hit!

When the opening show was over, Alice, Eartha, and Paul were among the ones who received great recognition for their performances. Paul was thrilled when New York critic Walter Kerr singled him out as, "The funniest bit of the evening." Brooks Atkinson of the *New York Times* wrote that he had a hard time picking the best talent of the seventeen performers. He mentioned six of them by name, and among them was Paul Lynde, The critic of *The New York Daily Mirror*, along with many others, raved. Paul was ecstatic at seeing his name so many times in print, and they were praising his unique style and humor.

During a performance, Robert Clary recalled Paul's sharp, unscripted wit: a lady heckled from the balcony during all the skits and kept saying, "I don't get it." So Ronny Graham complained to the stage manager, who then called the police. When they arrived, they escorted her out as Paul yelled out, "Now you're going to get it!"

As the weeks went on, Paul watched after each performance his fellow actors being greeted with bouquets of flowers and proud hugs from their families. He thought how surprised his parents would be if they could see him now. The show went to a theater in Chicago, and one evening after it finished, Paul was heading backstage. As he looked up, there was Marilyn. His high school girlfriend had come to see him perform. He was happy to see her. She congratulated him and they talked for a bit. When it was time for her to head home, she wished Paul success. The actor packed up his crutch and bandages, then exited the theater.

Paul was now making some money and bought two basset hounds. He named them Orville and Wilbur, after the Wright Brothers, whom he admired. His niece Nancy remembered those dogs as being such characters. The loveable long eared pups were spoiled by Paul and the three became a family. Paul did not want his dogs cramped up in a small apartment, so he went looking for a larger place. He liked living in Greenwich Village and found one he liked in the same area. He knew Robert Clary was living in a hotel so he let him have his former place. The rent was higher in this apartment so Paul began to cook at home to save the cost of eating out. He found he had a knack for cooking and invented his own recipes. He eventually invested in a cook book and found he loved being in the kitchen. He felt so confident as a chef, he began entertaining with small dinner parties. His friends were impressed and raved about the meals. Jimmy Russell, the captain of the dance team for *New Faces*, had dinner with Paul often. This seemed to be his first serious relationship with a man. Paul had kept his personal life as private as possible, but most of the cast knew they had been spending a lot of time together. Eventually things got complicated between Jimmy and Paul, so they went their separate ways.

Robert had not been close friends with Paul during *New Faces*, but was always grateful he had let him have his old apartment. As years went by, they crossed some roads together and their friendship grew. Robert bumped into Paul again in the 1970s, and Paul was very open to him about his lifestyle. Robert was in awe of his honesty.

New Faces of 1952 became one of the most successful revues ever. It ran for an astounding 365 performances. When the show closed, Eartha Kitt had become a huge star. Leonard then turned the show into a movie and it premiered in 1954, but he kept the title, *New Faces of 1952*, with most of the original cast, including Paul. Leonard was sure it would be as big a hit as the show, but it did not do well on screen.

Paul was disappointed. In spite of all the good press he had received from the Broadway version of *New Faces*, he was not getting offers to work. He needed money to pay his rent, so he performed in another revue, *Come as You Are*, in 1955. His stage fright was becoming severe, and he wouldn't talk to anyone before the show, but just kept repeating his lines. Again, the audience never had a clue because they only saw a talented, confident actor.

Paul couldn't believe he would be turning thirty in just a few weeks and still was not a star. Then Leonard Sillman called and asked him to help direct and write sketches for *New Faces of 1956*. Paul jumped on it. One of those new faces turned out to be Maggie Smith. Leonard had just brought her over from England, after having seen her in a revue in Oxford. He was raving about her, but when she came to the States, Paul said she was miserable. She would just sit there by herself in the studio every day.

Paul remembered Maggie as sitting on a chair, looking scared, and crying. He wanted to protect her, but he was too shy to let her know this. After days of walking past this silent, tearful female from Oxford, Paul turned to her and said, in his usual sarcastic voice, "Troublemaker." From that moment, they became close friends. He even directed her in one of the skits that he helped write. Paul and Maggie went out socially, and it was rumored that the two were dating. Sometimes Jan Forbes, Paul's good friend from college, and her husband Joel, would have dinner with Paul and Maggie. Jan noticed that Paul was very taken with Maggie. "He was shy about those feelings and never let Maggie know how he felt about her. They never became romantically involved." Years later Paul said, "That's one woman I could have married."

When Paul recalled his directing days with Maggie and the other cast members of *New Faces of 1956*, he admitted he was a terrible director because he wanted everyone to say the lines the way he would do them. He decided to stick to acting.

In 1957, Paul worked with another talented cast while filming *Ruggles of Red Gap*. It was originally a musical on Broadway and told the story of a western rancher who wins a butler in a British poker game. It was being filmed for television and would air on NBC. The movie starred Jane Powell, Michael Redgrave, Peter Lawford, Imogene Coca, and David Wayne. Paul played the part of Charles Belknap-Jackson.

Buddy Bregman, who arranged the music for this ninety-minute television episode, said:

> It was great fun working with Paul Lynde and also Sir Michael Redgrave and Jane Powell. There is a scene in the movie where Sir Michael recited The Gettysburg Address as he was leaving the Wild West, and Buddy said that scene "screams every day with Paul Lynde." Janie [Jane Powell] and I shared a Limo to rehearsal and taping to NBC Brooklyn studios every day for three months with Paul. I have never had more fun than that on any show. Paul would just say the most hilarious things; we laughed sooo much we could hardly speak.

Buddy orchestrated the score for movies such as the *Pajama Game* and *Crime in the Streets*. Buddy said:

> I have worked with every comedian in the world, Paul Lynde still is the funniest person I have ever known in my whole life, much less worked with! He was an absolute HOOT! Every night [During the filming of *Ruggles of Red Gap*] I went back to my hotel aching from laughing. We could hardly walk after a day with him. I shared a limo with him and from the beginning of each day until late at night — we all ate dinner together as well — we were crying we were laughing so much. His humor was unbelievable.
>
> Audrey Hepburn was in the next studio, doing Maerling, with hubby Mel Ferrer in #3 and every moment I could sneak out, I did to be with her. I finally got her to come into our studio and she screamed with laughter as Paul did her as The Princess in *Roman Holiday* — outrageously — camped about so much that when Mel came in, obviously not happy that she was there with me, Paul sidled up to him and in a trés butch manner and in keeping with the western theme of our show said, "Whatcha gonna do about it pardner?!" And then skipped off. It was and he was hilarious.
>
> Jane Powell will bear all of this, as she was at the wildest dinner with us at a steak house on Second Avenue. Paul would freak out when the waiters would ask for everyone's autograph but his. One time he ran after a waiter with a butter knife in his hand and into the kitchen screaming, "Your kids know me — they know who I am!" He then came back to the table breathing hard and 'powdered' his face with his steak! It was so wild and it lasted over four weeks!

That same year, Paul repeated his performance of *New Faces of 1952* in Miami, Florida, at the Cocoanut Grove Playhouse, where he enjoyed the beach and sunned himself whenever he had a chance. He then traveled to Missouri to perform in *Irene*. He finished that year in Kansas City as Vivian Budd, a butler, in *Panama Hattie*.

Paul returned to New York with some money in his pockets, and he used some of it for a trip to Canada. The plane had to make a fuel stop in Gander, and as it was taking off again, he and the passengers heard a startling noise and then they smelled rubber burning. The stewardess and staff were screaming and swearing in French. Paul did not know what anyone was saying. The plane landed safely, but Paul told a newspaper reporter, after that experience, he would only fly American planes. "Because if someone yells, 'we're crashing,' I want to understand them."

The funny faces and the acid wit that was delivered with such unusual inflections were still getting noticed, but at a snail's pace. It was 1958, and Broadway was still the pinnacle of fame, but Paul had no luck getting back on the big stage since *New Faces of 1952*. He was promised a role in a Broadway show called *Jack in the Box*, but it never panned out. He hadn't been offered any more directing jobs or writing opportunities either, since *New Faces of 1956*. He had talent; he just couldn't find where he fit in.

The Golden Age of Television was also exploding. The movie industry began installing bigger screens and better audio in their theaters to compete with this home entertainment in a box that almost every American was buying. At the time, there were three main networks, which all had hit shows: ABC had *The Wonderful World of Disney*, hosted by Walt Disney, along with *American Bandstand*, a hit show for teenagers dancing to rock and roll hosted by Dick Clark; NBC had *The Tonight Show* and *Dragnet;* and CBS had *I Love Lucy* and *The Ed Sullivan Show*. Paul learned some of these shows were getting over 40,000,000 viewers. This was more exposure than Broadway would ever get. He needed to be seen regularly on the screen of that box that was sitting in almost every living room in the country.

When the producers at *The Phil Silvers Show* called Paul and asked him to be on an episode, he couldn't get to the studio fast enough. That show had grabbed *three* Emmys for the best comedy series. Phil Silvers had played Sergeant Bilko of the United States Army, who was always trying to find ways to get rich quick and involved his soldiers in all his schemes. Paul played a desk clerk in the episode "Bilko's Big Woman Hunt," which aired on November 5, 1958. He appeared in two episodes of that show; than he had to find more ways to pay his bills.

The unemployed actor was approached to put the skits he had written and performed in *New Faces* along with some of his night club acts on an album. He thought it would certainly do well. One year later, Columbia Records came out with his live recording: *Paul Lynde Recently Released*. It began with "The Trip of the Month," his seven-minute monologue that got him noticed in *New Faces of 1952*. He followed it with "The Family Just Across the Moat," in which Paul played a mother who was just released from an institution. He cackles like a witch, while telling "her" son to wipe his feet, all four of them, and then tells him to go out and play in traffic.

The second track was called "Few Odd Odes," a bunch of morbidly funny poems written and recited by Paul. One of them was for a terminally ill friend in the hospital. It's called "Cheer Up."

There are roses in bloom,
In my hospital room.
Hear the bird in my window singing a song:
Cheer up, cheer up, you haven't got long...

The friend passed away while reading it. The artist's dark humor didn't hold up its appeal without his physical animated gestures and grimacing faces. The live album died on the shelves, and then his phone went dead too.

While performing in *Visit to a Small Planet* at the Bucks County Playhouse in New Hope, Pennsylvania, disaster struck. Paul was having his usual bout of stage fright before curtain time, petrified that he would forget his lines no matter how many times he had done the same show. He always managed to summon up the courage and get out there and pull it off. Not that night, though. In an article titled, "The Nervous Nellie of the Networks," in *TV Guide* magazine, Paul described how he walked on stage and no words came out of his mouth. His prompters called out his lines, but he stood there frozen for five unending minutes. The audience froze with him. The actors on the stage tried to cover for him, but the scene was not working. Another two full minutes past, still not a sound. The decision was made to bring the curtain down. The speechless actor headed back stage, humiliated. He wanted to walk out and never have anything to do with acting again. The producer and some of the cast reminded him he was meant to be an actor; this was his dream. After much convincing, Paul headed back on stage. He picked up where he left off and he didn't miss a beat. When the play was over, he received an ovation from the audience.

He continued with the theater circuit and next played Paul Anderson in *Season in the Sun*. In July, he headed to Long Island and appeared in the revue *Dig We Must*, with Alice Ghostly at the John Barrymore Theater in East Hampton. He was getting paid regularly, and he enjoyed having money in his pocket. The next character he played was Maxwell Archer in *Once More, With Feeling*, in Washington, D.C. He was now well-known in the theater industry, and a respected actor, but it was not enough for him.

When summer stock ended, Paul returned to his apartment in New York. He continued to go on auditions, and then raced home and stayed glued to the phone. He had been receiving much praise from critics and was frustrated as to why he wasn't being asked to do something big. When his phone rang and it was one of his friends, Paul sounded annoyed as he said, "Oh, it's you." He was also bothered again by the way he looked: his weight had gone back to over 200 pounds. The last thing he wanted was to be known as the "fat comic." He began to lose all his ambition. He stopped going on auditions. He stopped reading the cast calls in the paper.

Then, a huge break: he was asked to perform his "African Trip" monologue on *Toast of the Town*, which in 1955 was officially changed to *The Ed Sullivan Show*. This lead to more visibility on television, along with good pay; and Paul made appearances on *The Red Buttons Show* and *The Martha Raye Show*. On a sitcom called *Stanley*, he played the voice of hotel-chain owner Horace Fenton, who was never seen but only heard over a loudspeaker. This show, broadcast on NBC in 1956, starred Buddy Hackett and Carol Burnett, but was cancelled after several months. Nothing more came his way, and the actor worried again. He wished he had someone special in his life that he could talk to about it. He began to eat less and lost almost thirty pounds, hoping this would help his career and his non-existent love life.

Paul had been sure *New Faces* would have his name up in lights by now. He was sick of waiting by the phone for offers that never came. He met up with some of his actor friends from summer stock for drinks one night. One of the guys told him he had found an agent and was being set up for an audition. Paul listened, swallowing the last of his drink, and began showcasing his wit. His friends were laughing, having a good time, when another friend joined them, announcing his new gig. Paul could not figure out how these guys, some of whom did not even go to school for acting, were landing roles before he was. As the night went on and more drinks were poured, his sarcasm became mean and personal. His friends were taken aback; they couldn't figure out what came over him.

The next afternoon, when Paul woke up in his apartment, he thought about how he had originally given himself five years to become rich and famous, and now nearly ten years had gone by. He was frustrated and, just like the two-year-old boy who was taken away from his mother and had to compete for attention, he couldn't cope anymore. He missed his mom and brother Cordy, and was almost glad that his father was not around to see his failure. He thought about Marilyn. His torment escalated from an internalized tantrum to a dark, descending doom. Even Carl Canker couldn't laugh this one off.

Though he felt terribly down, Paul pushed himself to show up at a party that week. His friends were talking to him, but he couldn't concentrate. During dinner, he excused himself to leave. His friend, Alice Pearce, pulled him aside and asked him what was troubling him. He told her he was thinking of ending his life. She understood his pain; she had felt lost and alone after her husband died. She told him how she had benefitted from therapy and urged Paul to get into counseling. He was so desperate; he agreed to make an appointment. When his therapist introduced herself, Paul recoiled; her name was Sylvia, the same as his mother's. She spoke gently and persuaded him to let her help.

At a time when seeing a shrink was not very "in," Paul was open about it — even to the press. He talked about his therapist Sylvia, by name, and said, "She saved my life." His phone was ringing more. His friends were calling to make sure he was okay. For once, he didn't seem too disappointed that these calls could be tying up his line for the call that he never gave up on — the one that would lead him to that big role that would make him famous. He had just hung up from talking to Alice when the phone rang again. He picked up the phone and, this time, on the other end was a little birdie…one that would fly him right to the top.

Mariane Maricle and Paul rehearsing as Mr. and Mrs. MacAfee for *Bye Bye Birdie.*

CHAPTER 5

Bye Bye Birdie, Hello Paul Lynde

"An actor should never undergo psychoanalysis."
PAUL LYNDE

"I just need to be working," Paul said to his therapist. Sylvia nodded. She was relieved the distressed man who entered her office just weeks before was no longer thinking about suicide. Paul lit a cigarette as he told her how he tried to be a serious actor at Northwestern, but when he recited Cyrano de Bergerac "the class laughed so hard that I was typecast into comedic roles." He was sure he just needed the right part and he'd be successful.

Sylvia asked him about his childhood and teen years. Paul admitted he was made fun of by the kids at school, even his brothers. He explained he weighed 260 pounds when he entered high school. They talked about how his mother over indulged him with food and how food played a role in his life. As their sessions continued, Paul talked about his stage fright and his fear of forgetting his lines or walking on stage and not getting laughs. Reluctantly, he touched on the significant people he loved and lost to early deaths: his brother and both his parents. He talked of Marilyn, who had married another man.

He had no love life and wanted the passion he had seen in his favorite movie, *Wuthering Heights*. He longed to feel how Heathcliff felt for Cathy. The way he felt she belonged to him, referring to her as "*My* Cathy." Paul told *Ohio Magazine* that he became inconsolable every time he watched it. He also related to Heathcliff's dark side that emerged after he lost the love of his life. Heathcliff had become cruel and mean, the way Paul could become with the effects of alcohol.

Paul was not very comfortable talking about himself. "An actor should never undergo psychoanalysis," he later told *People Magazine*. "The mystery of not knowing why is important to an actor, and should be kept that way." He told Sylvia that he didn't seem to have time to take care of his dogs, Orville and Wilbur, the way they should be. She suggested he give them away, which he did, with a heavy heart.

After months of sessions, the two discussed how his weight was part of the problem. It was crushing his self-esteem and limiting his career. Paul was determined to change all that. He paid the three dollar fee for the session and headed out. He liked Sylvia and did not want to disappoint her, so he skipped dinner that night, continued to eat less, and began to lose weight. Later that year, he was in a car accident and lost more weight. When he recovered, he continued to ferociously diet, practically starving himself, and he began to exercise. In less than two years, he would drop one hundred pounds.

Paul was in his apartment when his phone rang, with what he thought was good news for a change. He was told that Gower Champion had seen him perform, and he wanted him for a part in a new musical. Paul did not know who he was, but was excited for an acting job and agreed to read the script. Edward Padula was producing the new show called *Bye Bye Birdie*. It was based on the book *Let's Go Steady* by Michael Stewart, who also wrote the script for the play. It was the story of a sexy rock star, mirroring Elvis Presley, named Conrad Birdie. Like Elvis, this idol was being drafted into the army. One lucky girl was to be chosen from his fan club for that one last kiss. She would represent all his fans. Albert Peterson was his manager and Rose was Albert's secretary and girlfriend. The play's rock star would sing *One Last Kiss* to that teenage fan on a staged *Ed Sullivan Show*.

The musical had over a dozen song and dance numbers. Charles Strouse composed the music and Lee Adams wrote the lyrics. Champion Gower was both director and choreographer. Dick Van Dyke, who had just finished in his first Broadway appearance, *The Girls Against The Boys*, auditioned for the lead role of Albert, singing *Til There Was You*, and then he performed with a few dance steps. When he finished, Gower told him he got the part. Charles Nelson Reilly, who played Mr. Henkel in the show, later became Dick's understudy and filled in when he took vacations.

The script was sent to both Eydie Gorme and Carol Hanley — to play Rosie, the female lead — but they both turned it down. Chita Rivera arrived, considering the part. She had become a star with her performance as Anita in *West Side Story*. According to Chita, after she read the script, she didn't think it was so good. "Kids and telephones, who would relate.

I wasn't an Elvis Presley fan." Then Chita sat and watched the first act. "The music was fun and I watched the guys and I was taken by it. I *have* to do this," she told her agent. And she did.

There was a new character added, who wasn't in the original story: a frustrated father of the starstruck teen. Gower had Paul in mind for that part right from the start. When Paul read the script, his heart sank and his temper rose. It was just a few lines! He was insulted and thought, *I'm better than this.* He walked out.

Paul told Al Cohn of *Newsday* that Gower followed him and gently pleaded with him to stay in the play. Gower told the upset actor that the parents would be bringing their kids to see it and Paul's role would be someone they could relate to. The soft spoken director told Paul he was made for this part, and he would work on it and make it an important role. Though he had just met Gower that day, Paul felt he was genuine and took the gamble. He shook the director's hand and returned to the stage.

The show still needed a pelvis-wiggling rock star Elvis-type: Over 500 males auditioned for that part. According to Dick Gautier, he had been working a club and heard about the show from his agent. It was called *Going Steady.* When Dick got back to New York, he heard that Gower and the composer had seen him earlier at the Blue Angel, and so he decided to audition for the part of Conrad Birdie — which was believed to be a play on words for Conway Twitty. He got it.

Chita had first met Paul at rehearsal, and her first impression of Paul was that she had never seen anyone like him.

> His humor was on the edge: nervous, shaky. I was amazed at his timing; I screamed and yelled when I heard him. He played the father who had no control over anything and all he wanted to do was be on *The Ed Sullivan Show.* He was so funny. When Paul was saying his lines, on stage, I have never heard laughter so long.
>
> Paul had Gower in the palm of his hands. Paul's part was originally thirteen lines, but when Paul verbally attacked Randolph [the young boy who played his son] it was like, what kind of father was this, saying, "Don't touch me," to his own son? It was Paul, he stimulated Gower. The writing for his part kept extending. Paul actually created the character.

Now thirty-four-year-old and slim, Paul played the neurotic, uptight father who just wants "respect-respect I tell you," with amusing perfection. Kaye Medford played Mrs. Peterson, Albert's overbearing mother. Paul's wife was played by Marijane Maricle. Their daughter, Kim, was played by Susan Watson, and their son, Randolph, was played by Barry Pearl.

Paul sang a few numbers in the show including "A Hymn for a Sunday Evening," which was about him, as Harry McAfee, appearing on *The Ed Sullivan Show*. Later that year, Paul and some of the cast members actually performed that number on television on *The Ed Sullivan Show*, along with a few scenes from *Birdie*. Ed Sullivan did not appear in the Broadway play, but did appear in the movie version as himself.

Bye Bye Birdie opened on Broadway on April 14, 1960, at the Martin Beck Theater, and it was an instant box office smash. The cast was ecstatic when they received a standing ovation, and almost every paper contained rave reviews. Most of the critics were pleasantly surprised; just about everyone behind *Birdie* were unknowns.

Paul was feeling the success. Gower had been right; the parents enjoyed the show as much as the kids. Paul told Bart Andrews, in *TV Star Parade's* June 1976 edition, "I think my role had a lot to do with that and it wasn't in the original script. That was Gower's brilliance."

Kaye Ballard thought *Birdie* was a great success because of Paul. The way he sang "Kids," she said. "It was fresh and funny." Paul said he created some of the character from a gym teacher he had in high school, along with the way his father sounded at times. No one had seen anyone play a father quite like Paul did.

According to Chita, there was always laughter coming from his dressing room, but one day she heard him saying things that she did not like. She went to his dressing room and stuck one finger through his door and said, "Don't you *ever* speak that way to anyone again."

Back on stage, Paul expected everyone to have the same discipline for perfection as he did. He had zero tolerance for mistakes and he let it be known. One evening, a cast member was sick and there was no understudy for that part. Chita's husband at that time, Tony Mordente, stepped up to the rescue. Chita and Tony had met when they were both in *West Side Story*. For *Birdie*, he was one of Gower's assistants and he also knew the part of the one who was sick. Tony had also been a stage manager and knew all about the importance of timing. When the curtain went up, Tony was doing the original timing and was not aware that it had been changed. When the curtain came down, Paul did not react very kindly and said mean things to Tony. Chita stepped in. It was the first time she ever had a confrontation with Paul, or anyone, and she was quite shocked. She told Paul he was "terribly rude and ungrateful," explaining that Tony could not have known they had changed the timing. Paul got upset and angry, as was she. Time smoothed things out and, after the show ended, Chita would always send Paul messages with good wishes for him.

Paul had the reputation of being one of the funniest people in the world and sometimes the moodiest. Chita understood the complexity of many comedians. "Comedy is the hardest thing in the world. Comics, they're totally exposed, and they take it personally. Most comics want to be serious actors, as if comedy was not brilliantly serious."

Dick Gautier had first observed Paul at rehearsal and said:

> Paul was tense and nervous, but he hadn't been on Broadway since *New Faces*. He was a consummate professional…The only time I heard him blow a line was when he was supposed to say (just before the Ed Sullivan hymn) "Me? Harry MacAfee on *The Ed Sullivan Show?*" He transposed two letters and it came out as "Me? Mary HcAfee on *The Ed Sullivan Show?*" He was the only one on stage who didn't find it humorous.

According to Gene Bayliss, who knew Paul from Northwestern and was now assisting Gower with the dance numbers, Paul was talented, but appeared a bit egotistical; after all, he was the star of the School of Speech and off-campus Waa-Mu Production. He gave Gower and Mike Stewart a special talent; they recognized it and molded his part in the show to give them all a huge success. Gene created the telephone number, among others in the show. When he did the initial staging for "Kids," he based it on a Charleston movement, as he did with the music. When Gower saw it he said "make it simpler," which he did. The song "Kids" was originally intended to be sung by another cast member, but was later decided to be given to Paul. As Harry MacAfee, he runs around the house demanding respect. When his son says he respects him, the befuddled father tells the ten-year-old, "I don't want your respe-e-e-ect." And then breaks out, singing, "Kids." He made that song quite memorable.

According to Dick Gautier, the cast got along well for the most part. Paul was especially chummy with Kaye Medford, but he wasn't too keen on Dick. He brushed him off as if he was some teenage twerp, though he was nearly thirty years old at that time. Dick felt he didn't show him any respect. One night he dropped the big key at the end of "Honestly Sincere," and Paul freaked out, saying that he ruined his scene: the one that followed. Another time, Dick told him that Lucille Ball was in the audience, and he said, "Get out. I don't want to know who's out there!"

As it neared Tony time, Paul had hopes of owning a trophy. So many critics had raved about his performance. He was heartbroken when he saw so many from the show were up for a Tony, but he was not. He was especially perturbed at Dick Gautier, who had been nominated. Dick said Paul would not even talk to him for a while. About this time, Dick was to perform stand up at the Bon Soir, a popular nightclub in the village. He would be opening for a new singer named Barbra Streisand. Barbra told *Playboy* that when she auditioned there, she was already on the stage when she realized she forgot to dispose of her chewing gum. She took the wad of gum out of her mouth and stuck it on top of the microphone. This made everyone watching laugh, so they assumed she was auditioning for a comedy act. Then she opened her mouth and sang and was signed up fast.

According to Dick, Paul arrived at the Bon Soir and took a seat with some of his friends. He did not come to support Dick, but to sneer at him — he could not wait to see his *Birdie* co-star bomb on stage. Paul hoped Dick would feel the same humiliation that he had often felt when he did nightclub acts. Dick opened the show and the audience loved his act. To his surprise, so did Paul, who went backstage after the show and told him so. He apologized and explained how he hated doing stand-up. They were closer after that.

Everyone in *Birdie* did well and was becoming famous. Jan Forbes came to see her college friend in the musical, and after the show, they walked into Sardis for lunch. "When Paul walked in everyone stood up applauding and cheering for him," Jan said. Twelve years of struggle, times of depression, and grueling stand-up, paid off: he was finally a star.

Bye Bye Birdie was nominated for eight Tony Awards in 1961 and won for Best Musical, which named Michael Stewart, Charles Strouse, Lee Adams, Edward Padula, and L. Slade Brown. Gower Champion recieved two: one for Best Choreography and the other for Best Direction of a Musical. Dick Van Dyke won for Best Featured Actor in a Musical. Also nominated were Dick Gautier, Chita Rivera, sceninc designer Robert Randolph, and musical director Elliot Lawrence.

Dick Gautier later saw a very soft side of Paul when he ran into him while they were both working for John Kenley. Paul was doing a comedy and Dick was in *Music Man*. Dick had brought his four-year-old daughter, Chrissie, to the theater, and Paul loved her.

Paul was enjoying stardom. "My shrink told me there was nothing wrong with me that a job wouldn't cure," he said. Sylvia saw that working was very therapeutic for her patient. It was time for them to part, though he still had some intimacy issues that had not been resolved. He needed to learn to love himself off stage and to allow himself to be loved, not limit it to the faceless sounds of applause.

After a year, some of the *Birdie* cast moved on. Paul remained for all 607 performances until it closed in October, 1961. He would continue that role in 1963, when it was turned into a movie. Dick Van Dyke kept his part as Albert and Janet Leigh now played the part of Rosie. Many of Paul's lines were changed, along with some scenes. Paul was unhappy with the movie and did not think it compared to the Broadway show. "I didn't get one laugh from the movie version," Paul groaned, despite the fact that he received great reviews. Judith Crist, film critic for the *New York Herald Tribune* wrote, "...Mr. Lynde alone is worth the price of admission..." *Cue magazine's* Emory Lewis called Lynde "a great clown," and *Variety* wrote that he was "deserving of star billing."

What irked Paul the most was the new twenty-one-year-old actress who played his daughter in the movie, Ann-Margret. It did not help that she had attended his alma mater, Northwestern University, but had never graduated. Paul was only fifteen years her senior, and he had to have his hair dyed gray so he would look old enough to be her father. He told the press he thought the whole movie was centered on her. "So she could do her teenage-sex-bombshell act," Paul said. "It should have been called, 'Hello Ann-Margret.'"

About this time, Dick Van Dyke had attended a party with Paul. In *A&E Biography's: Off Center,* Dick recalled the time that Paul had heard that Hal Prince, the Tony award winning producer and director, was going to be at a party hosted by a mutual friend. Paul just had to meet him — he would surely want him in his next production. He begged the hostess to invite him, and when he showed up, Paul, who had been drinking, walked up to Hal Prince. Instead of words of admiration, he began calling him terrible names. Mr. Prince was horrified.

The next day, Paul was so remorseful and could not believe what he had done. He had to apologize to the man. An arrangement was made so Paul could do just that. When that time came, Paul was so nervous he had a few drinks, and then he had a few more. He arrived at the party where Mr. Prince was attending. Paul walked right over to him and did a repeat performance, firing insults at him again.

After that horrific scene, Paul worried that story would get around and destroy his chances in show business for good, but his performance as Harry MacAfee had the actor's phone ringing off the hook. He was

getting calls to appear on more television shows, including the very popular *Perry Como's Kraft Music Hall,* on which he appeared five times as
Perry's Pal.

Paul felt his troubles were finally over and the dark cloud that seemed
to hang over his head was moving on. He would, however, be involved in
a horrific incident that would not only impact his career, but would also
haunt him for the rest of his life.

Paul totally immersed as he studies his lines for *Bye Bye Birdie*.

PHOTO: DON HUNSTEIN © SONY MUSIC ENTERTAINMENT

From right to left: Barry Pearl, Paul, Marijane Maricle, Susan Watson and cast singing at rehearsal for *Bye Bye Birdie*.

PHOTO: DON HUNSTEIN © SONY MUSIC ENTERTAINMENT

Marijane Maricle and Paul Lynde practicng their lines as Mr. and Mrs. Harry MacAfee from *Bye Bye Birdie.*

CHAPTER 6

Uncle Arthur, Uncle Paul

"Hi ya Sammy"

One of the funniest and most famous characters known in the world of television in the mid-1960s was known as Uncle Arthur. That hilarious role, played by Paul, was actually made just for his personality. It became one of his most memorable characters in his career.

William (Bill) Asher, who directed this novel show, as well as serving as production and creative consultant, had cast his new wife, Elizabeth (Liz) Montgomery, as the star. She played a beautiful witch, who married a mortal and tried to live as an ordinary housewife by not using her supernatural powers. The show, of course, was *Bewitched*, which first aired on ABC in 1964.

Liz's character was Samantha Stephens and her mortal husband, for the first four seasons, was played by Dick York. Samantha had all sorts of magical relatives who would literally pop in and out of the newlyweds' lives, creating havoc with their spells. Though actor Dick York was first to play Samantha's husband and became known as the "first Darrin" by audiences, it was actually Dick Sargent who had originally been cast to play that part. He couldn't accept it though because by the time the studio got back to him, he had already committed to another project. That's when Dick York was given the role. However, after the fifth season, York had to leave the show because of a severe back injury that had occurred while filming a handcar scene in the 1959 film *They Came to Condura*. Dick Sargent took over and became known as the "second Darrin."

Bill Asher asked Paul to be in one episode in the first season, but not as Uncle Arthur. He played Harold Harold, a neurotic driving instructor, hired to teach Samantha to drive. This twenty-sixth episode was titled *"Driving is the Only Way to Fly,"* and first aired in March 1965. Liz thought Paul was hilarious and enjoyed working with him so much that she asked her husband to find a way to make him a regular on the show. That's when Bill created the practical-joking uncle — the brother of Samantha's mother, Endora, played by Agnes Moorehead. Uncle Arthur was named after Liz's maternal uncle, Arthur Cushner.

Bill had first worked with Paul in the 1950s, when he was directing *Colgate Comedy Hour*. He had his hand in directing many of the most popular shows at that time, including *Make Room for Daddy*, and *I Love Lucy*. He was both producer and director of *The Patty Duke Show* in the 1960s, where Paul had a role in one episode as Mr. Snell, in "The Genius." Bill liked Paul; he thought he was very funny and had tremendous talent. When Bill began his involvement in *Bewitched* in 1963, he had also been busy directing the movie *Beach Blanket Bingo*, starring Frankie Avalon and Annette Funicello. Paul was cast in that movie as an agent named Bullets, who managed a teenage girl, played by Linda Evans.

Paul debuted as Samantha's uncle in "The Joker is a Card," in October of 1965. Uncle Arthur said off-the-wall puns and played outrageous pranks on his television family. He would greet his niece with a waggle of his head and a "Hi ya Sammy," in his amusing voice — and he would usually appear out of nowhere. Once he showed up in a photo on her living room wall, and, in that voice and maniacal — almost sinister-like — laugh, said, "I've been framed." Another time his head popped out of a pot on her stove and he said, "I'm a stew away."

In the episode "The House That Arthur Built," Uncle Arthur was in love, but his girlfriend did not like his practical jokes, so she dumped him. He was crushed and began singing in an operatic voice. And "poof," he was suddenly dressed like Pagliacci, the famous sad opera clown. He sings, "Laugh clown laugh, even though no one knows your heart is broken."

Paul had already acquired fame in these past few years, and he was reaching new heights as Uncle Arthur. He appealed to adults, teens, and children. When he was out in public, kids would call out, "Hey Uncle Arthur!" and they would imitate his voice. Paul ate it up, and said he was amazed at the amount of recognition he received from that part, as he averaged about one episode a year on *Bewitched*. "They must run a lot of reruns," he said.

On the set, Paul would always crack Liz up during rehearsal. It became so bad one time that Liz could not speak her lines, and neither of the actors could contain themselves before the camera. They were so out of control that Bill finally threw his hands up and told everyone to break for an early lunch. Paul cherished working with Liz, until she became Serena, Samantha's spit-firing cousin. As Serena, she got to play something a little spicier than a proper housewife and got to wear short skirts, lots of makeup, and a black wig. She invented the character herself and Paul hated it.

Uncle Arthur was always given the best lines when he was in scenes with Samantha, but now this "Serena character," had quite a few funny quips of her own. That was when Paul would become antagonistic towards her. Liz always adored Paul and told *Advocate* magazine that when she became Serena, Paul would get competitive. She asked him what bothered him so much about Serena, "Is it her wild wardrobe? I'll let you borrow it any Saturday night!"

Paul continued with other projects during this time, and he was cast as the voice of Pumpkinhead in the animated movie, *Journey Back to Oz*. He worked with a great cast, including Liza Minnelli, who played the voice of Dorothy. (Her mother, Judy Garland had played the original role in *The Wizard of Oz*.) Ethel Merman was the voice of the wicked witch, and Margaret Hamilton, who was the witch in the original movie, was now the voice of Aunt Em. Other voices in the movie were played by Danny Thomas and Risë Stevens. The voice of Pumpkinhead was paid $500 for his role.

Paul also made an appearance on *The Jack Benny Show*. Paul played a veterinarian for one of Jack's alligators that was sick. Paul was a usual wreck before the show, but the host of the show laughed so hard during rehearsal, the guest actor was feeling a bit more confident. Jack thought of how Paul had come such a long way since he had first watched him struggling in a night club when he was first starting out.

Bewitched continued to be a hit show, and in 1966, Bill Asher won an Emmy for Outstanding Directional Achievement in Comedy for *Bewitched*. That same year, the show lost Alice Pearce, who played the nosy neighbor, Mrs. Kravitz. She had been Paul's longtime friend and was the one who had helped Paul seek therapy when he was depressed. She died of ovarian cancer at forty-eight years old.

Liz and Paul appeared together that year on *Hollywood Palace*, a variety show where Paul and Liz read "The Dagger Scene" from Macbeth. This time Paul played the straight man and Liz got the laughs. They performed "Darts," a sketch Paul cowrote for *New Faces of 1956*, in which Maggie Smith had played the female role. Liz and Paul would work together again in 1972, and were opponents on the popular game show *Password*, hosted by Allen Ludden.

In season five, Bill used one of the themes from *I Love Lucy*, which he had directed in 1952, titled "Job Switching." It was the popular episode in which Lucy and Ethel had to work in a chocolate factory, and they end up in one big chocolate mess. Similarly, in "Samantha's Power Failure," Uncle Arthur and Samantha's way-out cousin, Serena, had their magical powers taken away by the Witches Council and were forced to work in a chocolate factory. In that episode, the two were hired by Buck, played by Ron Masak, and he instructed his new employees to dip bananas into chocolate and nuts on a rapidly moving conveyor belt.

According to Ron, the cast had only one night to memorize the script. The scene had to be done in one take because they were using real bananas and chocolate. Liz was pregnant when she did that scene, and the smell of the chocolate was getting to her. Ron said, "No one else knew it at the time — she was a classy pro." In the script, Ron (as Buck) did an impression of Paul: After Uncle Arthur said, "What do I do if my nose itches?" Buck said to Uncle Arthur, imitating his famous voice, "Scratch it…on your coffee break." During the rehearsal of that scene, Paul asked Ron if that's how he was going to do it [imitate him]. Ron said that Bill liked it and thought it was funny. Paul scrunched up his nose and simply said, "He would." That episode was voted as one of the five funniest TV scenes by *TVLand*. For anyone wondering if Paul stayed in character after his scenes, Ron said, "He *was* Uncle Arthur."

Bill, Liz, and Paul often went out to dinner together, and those nights were usually a blast, especially after Paul had a few drinks. They spent more time laughing than eating, as Paul cracked remarks about what some particular woman in the restaurant was wearing or how she ate. Paul did it with good humor, and the surrounding people would often laugh along. Paul continued to order drinks, and soon his comicality was interpreted as malicious — the patrons went from feeling mirthful to hostile. Bill would have to defuse the situation. Though Bill and Paul shared many laughs, Bill also saw a serious side of his friend. He believed Paul could have done a dramatic role, because, he said, "He had that depth."

Bill and Liz often had their good friend over to their home for dinner. One evening, as Paul drove up the Ashers' driveway, a woman in the neighborhood recognized the star, and soon the anticipated quiet evening became complete chaos. Kids outside began chanting "Uncle Arthur, Uncle Arthur," and soon many neighbors were jamming their heads in the windows trying to get a glimpse of Paul.

In 1968, the fourth year of *Bewitched*, Marion Lorne, who played the bumbling Aunt Clara on the show, had a heart attack and died. Paul, who already had a phobia of death that began when he lost three family members in three months, was a little spooked that another cast member of *Bewitched* died. It bothered him so much that he was hesitant about doing any more shows — but he did.

In an episode titled "Twitch or Treat," a very special warlock came to Uncle Arthur's Halloween party. It was Willie Mays, who at the time was playing for the San Francisco Giants. In that scene, Darrin, (Dick York)

Paul as Uncle Arthur with Elizabeth Montgomery in *Bewitched.* COURTESY ABC/ PHOTOFEST

can't believe the baseball great might have magical powers and asks his wife if he's a warlock.

Samantha answers, "The way he hits home runs, what else?" After that scene was filmed, Paul, along with the entire cast and everyone involved on the set, lined up for Willie, who stayed to sign autographs — and that was real magic.

In 1972, *Bewitched* ended its eight year run; in 1974, Bill and Liz ended their eleven-year marriage. Paul was distraught over his two closest friends' break up, and he told a reporter, "Sometimes, I think you're better off not being married today," he said. "When you see your married friends split up, it's devastating."

One year later, Agnes Moorehead died, and twenty years later, the star of the show would pass away too. Liz died of colon cancer in 1995.

Another person Paul loved was gone. Dick York died of emphysema in 1992, and Dick Sargent of prostate cancer in 1994. Bill Asher lived to the age of ninety and died in the summer of 2012.

There were 254 episodes of *Bewitched*, and most people are surprised that Paul was only in eleven of them. Uncle Arthur is still voted as one of the most favorite of all Samantha's relatives, and reruns are still shown on TV today.

Uncle Arthur had a lot in common with Uncle Paul. According to his niece Connie, both were funny and loved playing practical jokes. Uncle Paul had two nieces and a nephew, born to his oldest sister, Grace. Her children were Nancy, Connie, and Cordy (named after Paul's brother who was killed in the war). His other nephew, Doug, had been adopted by his brother Richard and his wife. Helen never married, nor had children; neither did his brother Johnny.

After his parents had died, Paul continued to celebrate Christmas with his family in Mount Vernon, at his elder sister's home. "The house was on Sugar Street," Connie said. "We would have big family Christmas dinners. My mother, Grace, would do all the cooking. Helen and Johnny would be there when Paul arrived." He would step out of his limousine, arriving from New York with his arms full of presents for everyone in the family. Paul's favorite holiday was Christmas Eve; he liked the buildup of the night before. His mom always made turkey on Christmas and the tradition continued with Grace. As the extended family grew, Paul became a grand uncle to Nancy's five children. He added them to his Christmas gift list, and would also visit at Nancy's house when he was in town.

The family would sing carols together and Paul and his brother Johnny were always joking around. At times, Uncle Johnny was even funnier than Uncle Paul, both Nancy and Connie agreed. According to Nancy, Johnny and Paul ran together when they were younger. They were the closest in age and were always making everyone around them laugh. Paul, Johnny, and their high school friends would take a drive from Mount Vernon to Danberry, looking out for someone with their thumb in the air looking for a ride. When they found one, they would have the hitchhiker get into the car, and then they would all pretend to be deaf and mute — just for laughs. Other times, they would find out whose parents weren't home and then sell their furniture.

Paul especially enjoyed the company of his younger brother, who always made him laugh. He explained to a *Newsday* reporter that it wasn't just his humor; there was something funny about the sound of his voice. Paul knew they sounded alike, and he attributed that fact to his success of being able to make people laugh. Johnny saw every movie his brother was in. He would take a seat, and as soon as Paul was on the screen, he pulled out his camera and started snapping pictures. The people in the movie theater became annoyed and the manager would kick him out. Johnny would leave and find another theatre with the same movie and start snapping away again.

As Nancy became a teenager, she learned to play piano; and her uncles would come sit with her and play along. Cordy had a beautiful voice and could play piano by ear. Paul said he was the one who should have gone into show business.

When their uncle was living in New York, he would shop there for gifts to bring to his relatives. Among Connie's favorites were marionettes called Summer, Winter, Spring, and Fall from *The Howdy Doody Show*. On another visit to Ohio, her uncle brought her "Clarabelle" from that same show. It was the famous mute clown who never spoke until the very last show and only said, "Good-bye Kids."

Grace, Helen, and Nancy would get beautiful gowns from their brother. "The type you would wear to a premiere in New York or a fancy occasion," Connie said. Uncle Paul also brought Connie a Daniel Boone fringe jacket, and a coonskin cap with a tail. He brought his young nephew Cordy, the most wonderful tricycle with a red wagon attached. That tricycle ended up being very valuable years later.

The family was amazed how much Paul had slimmed down during the Broadway *Birdie*. He was doing well financially and had also just finished doing his first commercial for Instant Maxwell Coffee. Paul usually visited the family alone, but as the years went by he sometimes brought along his chauffeur or bodyguard. According to Connie, Paul was very respectful to the family. He kept his love life very private.

Nancy remembered when her uncle was first living in New York, he was struggling. It was about a year before *New Faces*, and Paul called his sister Helen and told him he was going to be in a revue called "*What's New?*" that would be coming to Cleveland. Nancy and her mother, Grace, along with Helen, drove to the Statler Hotel to see him. The cast would do a floor show, singing and dancing. It happened to be on Nancy's birthday, and, during intermission, the whole cast sang happy birthday to her. Paul had set that up as a surprise. He was always doing special things like that for the family.

On Wednesday, July 10, 1963, when Paul was thirty-seven years old, Mount Vernon declared a "Paul Lynde Day," to honor his achievements in the arts. It was a huge celebration and the streets were filled with fans, friends, his former classmates, teachers, and almost everyone who lived there. The town put together a parade for Paul, and afterward there was a reception.

When Mount Vernon High School put a new wing on the school, it was dedicated to Paul. One of his female friends from high school gave a huge party for him. His fellow Ohioans made him honorary congressman for his work for the heart foundation. When the Kenley Players brought their production, in which Paul starred, to Ohio, it was a guaranteed sellout. He was given the red carpet treatment, and it seemed that the majority of the state came out to see him. "When I do a show in Ohio, it's Judy Garland time," Paul told *TV Star Parade*, "It's very emotional and overwhelming."

Mount Vernon became a magical town on those nights. Huge crowds would gather to talk to Paul after the show and get his autograph. The family was very proud of him and saw how gracious he was to his fans; he would stop and talk to all of them, never refusing an autograph or a handshake. Sometimes Connie would have dinner for her uncle and the family at her house. Other times Paul would reserve a private room at a Polynesian restaurant nearby, so they could spend time with him alone.

In the summer of 1963, Paul said good-bye to his favorite city, New York, and moved to California. New York had Broadway and many acting opportunities, but it was time for him to go where MGM, Paramount, and most of the major motion picture studios were. He hoped to live one day among the movie stars, but for right now The City of Angels seemed like a good place to start. He rented a Spanish-style home on Phyllis Avenue in Los Angeles. Shortly after he was settled in, he flew back to Mount Vernon where he would join his roots for a special showing of the movie, *Bye Bye Birdie*. It was an extravagant night for the town and his family, and, once again, Paul showed his gratitude to all his friends and fans who showed up to support him.

Paul headed back to his new home in the golden state, where he still had family close by. Both Helen and Johnny had moved to Los Angeles before he did. Johnny worked as an accountant there, and he fixed clocks as a hobby. Paul invited his brother and sisters along with his nieces and nephew, who flew in from Ohio, to see a taping of *The Hollywood Squares*. He introduced his family to Charlie Weaver, Richard Crenna, Peter Marshall, and all the stars that appeared on the show that week; and then they dined together during the break.

In 1963, Paul was given the role as the sportscaster in Walt Disney's production of *Son of Flubber*, starring Fred MacMurray. Paul appeared in his next movie, *For Those Who Think Young*, which United Artists released in June 1964. It starred Ellen Burstyn and James Darren. Paul played Hoyt, part of a two-man night club act — the other man was Woody

Woodbury, who was known for his nightclub acts and played himself. The movie was about a group of teenagers whose favorite beach hangout was about to be shut down, so they blackmailed the owner in order to keep it open. That movie did well at the box office.

Woody Woodbury recalled:

> At Paramount, it was the most happy-go-lucky bunch I ever worked with. They were all young kids and I believe other than George Raft and Robert Armstrong, Paul and I were doubtless the oldest people on Stage 5! Nancy Sinatra, Bobby Denver, Claudia Martin (Dean's daughter) Pamela Tiffin, Jimmy (James) Darren, and Ellen McRae (later she became Ellen Burstyn and won the Academy award for *Alice Doesn't Live Here Anymore),* Tina Louise, we're all teenagers. Some of the beach kids were real preschoolers and fun to be around.

According to Woody, Paul was a consummate pro on the set.

> I believe anyone you ever speak to regarding his high degree of professionalism was that he possessed that one and most vital virtue: HE LEARNED HIS LINES! It makes it so much easier for everyone involved in any scene when the actors know their cues, their lines, and their movements on the set. Paul was a master at it. To the best of my recollection, he and I never did a re-take during the entire filming of "For Those Who Think Young." (If history ever proves me wrong on this, it'll be because I goofed — and not Paul.)
>
> He knew the movie business far better than myself and the only agitation I ever saw in him was identical to that of other cast principals when we had to stand and wait and wait and wait while another couple or group were being filmed and there were interruptions of one kind or another. Standing around and watching a scene being shot can be unnerving to everyone if there are a lot of retakes or technical problems. That's why Paul and I seemed to whiz right through our scenes — secretly watching him like a hawk enabled me to pick up and learn from him those very expressive gestures, eye movements, facial expressions, and all that sort of thing. He was, to use an old vaudevillian definition, a real "mugger." He had eyebrow, facial, and on-set contortions that the camera loved. Watch him in *Bye Bye Birdie* and you'll see him in rare form.

After the shooting, a few of the cast would go out together for dinner.

The few times we ate at Joe's he'd always be alone to meet Sue, [Woody's wife at the time].

Woody had one stand thing about Paul that he observed during their time together, and that was his diet. Paul told Woody of a quiet and small restaurant on Melrose named "Joe's Steak House." It was not far from Paramount's main gate. They usually met at Joe's for dinner, maybe five or six times during the time of filming. The standout part was how he raved about how great Joe's steaks were. But first the waiter would bring a large tray of huge ice-cold sliced raw onions, ice-cold bright red thick-sliced tomatoes, and king sized, ice-cold green, pitted olives, all in a row on ice-cold beds of romaine lettuce. There were actually ice cubes adorning the platter.

Well, Paul would immediately attack that platter. Without fail, he'd continue to extoll the great steaks we'll have just ordered, but he never gave up digging into those raw onions, tomatoes, olives, and romaine. Soon the big, thick, steaks arrived. Paul would take one or two bites of that while still devouring the ice-cold stuff, and then suddenly looking sad, he'd ask for a doggie-bag into which the waiter placed his steak.

According to Woody, neither he nor any human being who ever had dinner with Paul Lynde during the filming, ever saw him finish a steak. He told everybody on the set about Joe's Steak House and how terrific the sirloins were. All the time, he would be broadcasting to the world at large about the fantastic steaks at Joe's, but then proceeded to gorge himself with all the ice-cold goodies and never left room in his stomach for the main course. They wondered how he ever really knew if Joe's steaks were so sensational. He never ate one!

Paul was not big on small talk. However, he became fascinated, one night at dinner, when he learned about Woody's background. Woody recalled:

I had been a U.S. Marine Corps pilot in a couple wars, and Paul seemed stunned to discover and was quite surprised at that. In turn, I was surprised when he expressed great interest in the Corps and knew so much about it. I was a replacement pilot in Gregory "Pappy" Boyington's "Blacksheep" Squadron. And I hasten to say I was no hero. I was selected to fly fighter planes in that squadron long after the "Blacksheep" had captured the verve and nerve of Boyington's antics and subsequent adoration by the public. Paul displayed honest amazement when he discovered I flew Jet fighters in Korea also.

Paul showed genuine surprise that I had done these things. Other than himself and Howard W. Koch, Jr., who produced the film, I don't believe anybody else in the entire cast or production group ever knew I was a military Marine Corps flyer. Paul wanted to know how cold it was in the jets, did they have heaters up at thirty thousand feet, and how many times were you hit by anti-aircraft fire — all such as that.

Paul was already well up the ladder to stardom, and I was a mere cabaret lounge performer-host so as quickly as it dawned upon me that the reason he was climbing by leaps and bounds up that ladder of screen and television success was that he knew everybody else's lines in the script as well as his own. The guy was a gem to work with.

As hilarious and memorable as Paul's presence on television always was, he was referred to as "what's his name, that funny guy." He had been appearing in several movies including the romantic comedy *Send Me No Flowers*, which starred Doris Day, Rock Hudson, and Tony Randall. In that movie, Rock Hudson played a hypochondriac who thinks he is dying. He makes an appointment to buy a cemetery plot. He meets with Mr. Akins, played by Paul, who cheerfully tells him, "When you're ready, we're ready."

A few years later, Paul co-starred in *How Sweet It Is*, with James Garner and Debbie Reynolds. He was also appearing on some of the most popular sitcoms of that time: *The Munsters*, as a nearsighted doctor; *F-Troop* as a singing Mountie whose motto was "We always get our man;" *That Girl; I Dream of Jeanie;* and *The Beverly Hillbillies*. People were imitating him with some of his signature lines, like, "Oh, my go-o-o-o-odness" and "Tha-a-a-t's disgu-u-u-usting." With so much exposure, he just couldn't understand why no one could remember his name. That is until he would be a guest on a very different kind of television show, one that would catapult him to overnight fame.

"Brothers." Johnny and Paul in Los Angeles.
COURTESY OF NANCY NOCE AND CONNIE RICE

"Festivities for Paul Lynde Day" (1963). Paul with Grace (Paul's sister), and her husband Ralph. PHOTO COURTESY OF NANCY NOCE AND CONNIE RICE

Paul's sister Grace, and her daughter Nancy's children: Kirk, Lisa, Suzy, (Great) Uncle Paul, and Todd Noce (in front) at Nancy's home Christmastime, Mt. Vernon, Ohio (1967). PHOTO COURTESY OF NANCY NOCE

Paul (center) dining out with his family and friends at Kahiki Polynesian restaurant in Columbus, Ohio. On the right: Grace (his sister), Connie (Rummel) Rice (his niece), and Ralph Rice. On the left: Nancy Noce (his niece), and Bill Noce. COURTESY OF CONNIE RICE AND NANCY NOCE.

Uncle Paul, Todd, Suzy, and Rob Noce — Christmas at Paul's home. COURTESY OF NANCY NOCE

Paul and Alfred having a conversation, while his great nephew listens. COURTESY OF NANCY NOCE

Paul and his great niece, Shelly (Rice) Thompson. COURTESY OF NANCY NOCE

Paul Lynde with his famous smirk, about to deliver a side-splitting joke on *The Hollywood Squares.* COURTESY NBC/PHOTOFEST

CHAPTER 7

Hollywood Scares and Squares

"I've just lost my career..." PAUL LYNDE

"I shot three people, drowned one, and stabbed another. It was so much fun," Paul told a *Lakeland Ledger* reporter. He had finally been cast in a serious role. He said not one comical line, nor did he make any of his amusing facial gestures in the black-and-white detective television show, *Burke's Law*. Paul played Arthur Clark, a man who kills his own brother in "Who Killed Cable Roberts?" The episode aired on October 4, 1963. The producers were pleased with his performance, and he was a guest star two more times — each time playing a cold killer. (In one of those episodes, the detective finds a feather at the crime scene and wonders if the murderer is a chicken plucker. By the end of that show, it is the feathered pillow that Paul used to silence his gun that gets him caught.)

He told his good friend Kaye Ballard that he was planning to pursue more serious roles, as that was his original intent from age five. According to Kaye, she watched Paul in those episodes of *Burke's Law* and just couldn't see him serious. Paul was getting known as the funny guy with the funny voice. She just didn't understand why he was so intent on doing serious acting. She told her friend, "Paul, they know you; you've established yourself." He didn't want to believe that.

He did get another small role that began on the serious side, on the variety show *Hollywood Palace*, in 1965. Each week, a different star would host the show. On this particular show, Fred Astaire was the host and he introduced Paul as a "Refreshing and versatile actor-comedian." In the skit, Paul attempts to stop a woman (played by Carmen Phillips) from jumping off a bridge.

Thirty-nine-year-old Paul always wanted to have a series of his own. Bill Asher knew this, and together they began working on a new pilot for ABC. Paul would star as *Sedgewick Hawk-Styles: Prince of Danger*, a Victorian investigator. The show was set in the late 1900s, and Sedgewick has been assigned a mission from Queen Victoria, who he believes is really a man, to find the stolen Magna Carta. Bill thought it was a wonderful show and really funny. The busy producer and the actor had also just finished shooting another episode of *Bewitched*. This was the first time Paul played his new character, Uncle Arthur. When the filming of that episode was complete, he decided he was in need of a weekend getaway. So on July 17, 1965, Paul invited a friend, twenty-four-year-old Jim (Bing) Davidson, to spend the weekend with him in San Francisco. Jim was a bit actor who was in the 1963 movie *Move Over Darling*, starring Doris Day and James Garner, and just three months prior had a role in another movie, *Take Her She's Mine*.

Paul had booked a room at the Sir Drake Hotel. He and Jim went out for a night on the town. After a night of drinking, Paul had arrived back at the hotel around 2:30 a.m. and went up to his room. Jim followed, but was acting up in the lobby, so hotel security escorted him to his room about fifteen minutes later. Paul saw his friend come in, and later Jim said, "Watch me do a trick." Then Jim opened the window and hung from the ledge.

A policeman driving by noticed a man dangling from the hotel window. He radioed for the fire department while his partner bolted out of the patrol car and raced through the hotel lobby and up to the eighth floor. The papers reported that witnesses watched in horror as Davidson tried to pull himself up three times. When Paul realized Jim was in trouble, he dashed over to the window and grabbed him by the wrists. He told his friend to grab him around the neck, but Jim kept slipping. A witness said Paul frantically tried to help. Jim couldn't hang on, and he fell eight stories to his death.

Paul was traumatized having just watched Jim fall to his death. He was also sure this incident would destroy him. "I've just lost my career," he said. The policemen told him not to worry, they had seen everything. The coroner report showed the young man had been drinking heavily before the prank, and his death was listed as accidental. Jim's body was shipped to his hometown in Hastings, Nebraska. Paul told a reporter he received a beautiful letter from Jim's parents, explaining what happened was inevitable.

Paul returned home and obsessed over what would happen now. He knew some of his friends must have heard, even though it had only been in a few papers, but no one reached out to him. When his longtime friend Jan Forbes heard about the incident, she was very concerned about the effects it would have on her dearest friend. She wrote him a long letter and mailed it from Pittsburgh. Paul's response was, "I knew I could count on you. You're the first person I ever heard from." Paul told her that he wasn't really paying that much attention to Jim that night. Jim had been showing off and then he hung from the ledge. Paul told her it was the worst thing that ever happened to him.

"He was crushed!" Jan said. The story was squashed except for a few newspapers. It could have ruined him. One of those papers had a photo of Paul with a caption that read: "Actor falls to death." When Paul's sister saw that, she fainted. She thought it was her brother that fell to his death.

Paul returned to the Hollywood life and kept himself busy with his new pilot, playing the brilliant detective. Paul said it was his favorite character. The show was scheduled to air in 1966, but suddenly ABC decided to drop it. They were replacing it with *The Pruitts of Southampton*, starring Phyllis Diller. CBS then took on Paul's sitcom but, before it aired, they too reneged. Paul could not believe what was happening. Bill had suspicions the networks got wind of the incident that Paul was involved in and thought it was too risky to chance. Paul thought it was the best work he ever did. Bill agreed, but there was nothing they could do about it. When some of Paul's friends watched the print of the show, they told him they laughed throughout the whole show. He sadly told them he didn't want to hear about. He thought this role showed he had real acting talent, outside of playing somebody's distraught father.

One month following these disasters, the death cloud continued to plague Paul. He received a call that his youngest brother, Johnny, was dead. He had been lying in a Los Angeles hospital for a year, after a car accident. Johnny had never recovered and eventually died from a heart attack. He was only thirty years old. This was the brother who was such a fan, who used to take pictures of Paul on the screen in the movie houses and made him laugh growing up. Two of Paul's brothers were now gone. Johnny's body was flown back to Mount Vernon, where Paul returned once again, this time for a fourth family funeral.

Paul's eldest niece, Nancy, was at the funeral parlor to pay her respects to her Uncle Johnny. When Paul walked into the room, he was amazed and touched to see who else was there. "Some of the oldest nuns, who took care of Paul and Johnny, when they were little, came to the funeral," Nancy said. "When Paul saw them there, he just broke up. These women, who were very old now, came to honor Johnny and Paul."

After the services, Paul headed back to L.A. Half his family was now gone. Years later Paul explained that "shock was a good thing" and that it was shock that kept him working and not falling apart when he lost his parents and brothers. "If my humor became a little macabre, any wonder why?" he said to Jane Ardmore in an interview for *Weight Watcher Magazine.*

Realizing his own mortality, Paul had a will drawn up on Oct 1, 1965. His wishes stated he be cremated and buried with his mother, father, and brothers — though later, he did say he'd like his ashes dropped over New York. His sister Helen was to receive his art collection and his dog, and everything else was to be split equally between her and her sister Grace. His brother-in-law was to receive his clothing and jewelry. He left $10,000 for his nephew to use for college.

Paul was cast in a romantic comedy movie in 1966, *The Glass Bottom Boat.* It had a slew of stars including Doris Day, Rod Taylor, Arthur Godfrey, Dom DeLuise, and Dick Martin. Paul played a suspicious security guard who was determined to prove that Doris was a Soviet spy. In one scene, he wore a blue satin dress with a matching colored bow, which he wore in a red beehive-styled wig.

"I had a drag scene in *Glass Bottom Boat,*" Paul told a newspaper reporter as he laughed. "I wore an elegant gown. Everybody went wild! Doris came over and looked me up and down and told me, 'Oh, I'd never wear anything that feminine." Though both Paul and Dom DeLuise did *The Glass Bottom Boat* together, *The New York Times* singled out DeLuise, who went on to do other movies and became a regular in many directed by Mel Brooks. Paul later told the press he would like to perform in *Macbeth…* as Lady Macbeth.

In 1967, the determined actor tried again with another pilot, *Manley and the Mob,* but it never sold. He played a detective, very much like the one in *Get Smart.* Actor Nehemiah Persoff was asked what it was like working with Paul and said, "He was very much closed in within himself. I don't think anybody knew him." Paul had his hopes up again when he was cast in a movie called *Silent Treatment* in 1968, with Forrest Tucker, Phyllis Diller, and a bunch of other well-known actors, but it was never released. He was beyond frustrated, but still never turned down any offer. He said when he picked up the phone he never said hello, he answered, "Yes I can."

Game shows were big on television in the sixties and Paul popped up on quite a few of them. Heatter-Quigley had produced a few of them including *The Celebrity Game,* and *Funny You Should Ask. The Celebrity*

Game had six celebrities, each of whom was asked the same question, and the contestants had to guess their answers. On one show, the host asked Paul, "Would you do a nude scene in a movie?" Paul answered, "No, never...I lose the power of speech just taking a shower." He broke up the audience, the host, and the celebrity panelists. The same question was asked of Abby Dalton, Michael Landon, Jan Murray, Zsa Zsa Gabor, and Gypsy Rose Lee, who were suddenly all camera shy.

Paul finished filming *Under the Yum Yum Tree,* which starred Jack Lemmon, Carol Lynley, Dean Jones, Edie Adams, and Imogene Coca. Jack had done so many films and had starred in such great movies as *The Apartment, The Days of Wine and Roses,* and *Irma La Duce.* He won an Academy Award for Best Actor in a Supporting Role in *Mister Roberts* in 1956, and later, one for Best Actor in a Leading Role in *Save the Tiger.* Paul told *Newsday* that Jack, who did not like *Yum Yum Tree,* was feeling so down about doing the film that Paul talked to him every day before they began shooting, repeating to him what a great actor he was, just to keep him going. In this 1963 romantic comedy, Jack played a swinging bachelor, who managed an apartment building with only female tenants. Yet *Yum Yum Tree* did so well at the box office that it helped make Jack the biggest movie star in America. Paul was not happy with the film either, though *The New York Times* wrote: "...Paul Lynde and Imogene Coca are killing as custodians."

About this time, Ralph Story, who was an American television and radio personality, and also a well-known Los Angeles newscaster, was making an educational film about the need for public transportation in L.A. The film opened with Paul saying, "I'm a professional skeptic. I trust no one," and he held up a sign that read: *Public Transportation, who needs it?* Paul joined the opposing crowd who challenge Story's law: Everyone benefits from public transportation. That film was distributed in 1968, to schools and libraries by The Southern California Rapid Transit District. That law never passed.

That same year, a new game show was about to make its debut, another Heatter/Quigley production, called *The Hollywood Squares.* It was played like tic-tac-toe, except there were nine celebrities sitting in each box on a scaffold of three tiers. To earn their X or O, contestants would pick a star and then had to figure out if the star was bluffing or not when they answered questions read by the emcee, Peter Marshall.

Peter had nine slots in his desk that coordinated with the position of each celebrity on the grid. Before each show, some celebrities were given a list that the audience did not know existed. This list had the jokes to match the questions they were asked. They were never told the correct answer, just the funny lines to go with them.

The first show had Rose Marie, Wally Cox, Cliff Arquette, Sally Field, Agnes Moorehead, Nick Adams, Abby Dalton, Morey Amsterdam, and Ernest Borgnine. There were different celebrities on each week. Paul was a guest for its first two years and did not sit in the center. Sometimes he sat in the right bottom square next to Rose Marie, who, as a child singer, was known as "Baby Rose Marie," and went on to vaudeville and theatre. She appeared on many television shows and is most likely best known for her roles on *The Dick Van Dyke Show* and *Squares*. Paul loved to tease her. He was asked by Peter on this game show, "As we know, Paul, instead of letters, the Chinese drew pictures. What would a woman and a broom stand for?" Paul answered, "If it's flying, it's Rose Marie." She was always a good sport about it, and she referred to Paul as her buddy.

Rose Marie's favorite joke she ever heard Paul say was when Peter asked him, "You are driving seventy miles an hour and suddenly your brakes go, what should you do?"

Paul answered, "Honk if you love Jesus."

The audience and home viewers could not get enough of his unique humor. More side-splitters were produced when Peter asked him, "What fictional character ran around saying, 'I'm late, I'm late?'"

Paul answered, "Alice, and her mother's just sick about it." After the laughter died down, he then had to give a serious answer for that same question. He hated having to think on his feet. "I was very insecure the first year," Paul said, "I'm a script-man, I like to know what I'll be doing." He was also sure the contestant and the viewers would think he was not too bright if he didn't get the answers right, so he kept up on current events. He was well educated in art, cooking, and many other subjects, but always worried about how he came across.

That year, *The Dean Martin Show* was going into its fourth season, and the show would have a new theme and title. It would now be called *The Comedy Hour*, which featured the Golddiggers, twelve beautiful young females who sang and danced around Dean. According to the book *Backstage at The Dean Martin Show*, Greg Garrison, who was both producer and director, wanted Shecky Greene to star in the show, but Shecky turned it down. Greg had his second choice in mind: Paul Lynde. Paul jumped at the chance for more exposure on the tube. He fussed about some of the scripts and was infuriated when he had to work with Barbara Heller because she would not memorize her lines. Adding to his already frazzled nerves, he was having to wing it with Dean, who often did not come to the rehearsals. The bright spot for Paul was that he loved working with Joey Heatherton and got along well with Frank Sinatra Jr. and most of the other stars. Though he continued to complain about some of his lines, he stuck it out and became a semi-regular on the show.

Meanwhile, Jackie Mason, who had been sitting in the center square for one taping of *The Hollywood Squares* that year, was scheduled to tape again the next day, and as he was leaving, producer Les Roberts called out to him, "See you tomorrow."

According to Les, Jackie said, "I don't think so; I'm too big for the show."

Les had to scramble to find someone to take his place and was given three names to call: one of them was Paul Lynde. Paul was available and was seated in the center of the tic-tac-toe board, which was the most likely square to be called on in every game. The show had a viewership of over 12 million, and Paul helped make *Hollywood Squares* — and himself — household names. The writers had fun writing for Paul and often hinted at his homosexuality. For example: Peter asked him, "You're the world's most popular fruit. What are you?"

Paul replied, "Humble."

Peter also asked Paul: "True or false Paul, research indicates that Columbus liked to wear bloomers and long stockings."

Paul answered, "It's not easy to sign a crew up for six months."

He became a regular along with Vincent Price, Rose Marie, George Gobel, Jonathan Winters, and Karen Valentine. The other squares would be filled in by different celebrity panelists each week. Paul said some of them — like Ethel Merman — were a wreck as they waited to be called on. Paul advised the new players to be themselves and just have fun. Paul would also get nervous, not knowing if his jokes would go over well. He said that the contestants did not care if he got a laugh — they just wanted to win the refrigerators.

The producers of *The Hollywood Squares* decided to add a Saturday show for kids in 1969, called *Storybook Squares*. It was the same game, but the contestants were children and all the panelists had to dress up like storybook characters. At first Paul thought it might be bearable. After all, he knew he had a special connection to teenagers, ever since *Birdie*. He also received more letters than any other star at the time, from parents whose children were mentally challenged. He was told, in the letters, that their kids reacted to his facial expressions. (Paul promoted "hire the handicapped" in a public service announcement.) This new show might add more kids to his fan base and the costumes might even be fun to wear...so he thought. On one of those shows, Paul had to dress as the

Evil Queen from *Snow White*. He hated it, mostly because he was ribbed so much about him actually being an evil queen. *Storybook Squares* only stayed on the air for four months.

Occasionally, the celebrities dressed up in costumes for the nighttime show. Paul appeared as Frankenstein's monster with the big forehead, a green face, bolts sticking out of his neck, and bulky large shoes. On these theme shows, the stars did a walk on. Whether it was those shoes, the huge mask, the stairs, or the wine he might have drunk at the dinner break, Paul walked out like Jack Benny, with his hand on his hip — and then lost his balance. The next thing seen is the back of his shoes — he had fallen flat on his face. When he made it to his cubicle, Florence Henderson was seated next to Paul and she, in fun, threw a glass of liquid at him. Paul, who never left his cubicle when on camera, stood up, went over to Florence's cubicle, and playfully attacked her.

Some of the stars who dressed up for these shows were: Wally Cox, who once dressed as Davey Crockett; Nanette Fabray was the old woman who lived in the shoe; and Rosemarie was Pocahontas. Sandy Duncan dressed up as Mrs. Satan; George Gobel dressed as Confucius; and on this particular night, Paul was Narcissus. He wore a Goldilocks-type wig with long, blonde banana curls and wore a white toga.

Peter then asked "Narcissus" a question: "What is the worst thing you can say to your hairdresser?"

Then Paul gave an answer that was bleeped — the first time ever.

Suddenly, someone put on the song, "I feel pretty, oh so pretty, I feel pretty and witty and gay." Paul looked so annoyed as he tapped his fingers and gave a look like "I'll get you later for this." Peter laughed so hard he couldn't even get the words out for the next question. "This is going to cost me the Emmy again," he said, trying to stifle his laugh. Peter went on to win four Emmys for his outstanding work as a game show host.

Paul was content when he had fellow celebrities that he liked on both sides of his square. He was especially happy when Karen Valentine became a semi-regular on *Squares*. The Emmy-award-winning actress had starred in *Room 222*, and she had appeared on many television shows and also several movies. There was something about Karen that tugged at Paul's heart. They had become very close when they were making the television movie *Gidget Grows Up*, which aired in 1969. She was seated right next to the center square, and the two were always giggling and talking to each other. Later, Karen had to move to the top tier because some of the audience thought they were giving each other answers.

The stars were all seated in their boxes one afternoon, getting ready to tape the next show, when all of a sudden the tic-tac-toe board began shaking. The lights were flickering. It was a tremor, and everyone on the set ran out. Nervous, chronic dieter headed right for the candy machine. "I couldn't get the dimes out fast enough," he later said. He looked at Karen, who was next to him, said, "Oh, you're too young to go."

Peter Marshall, who had spent so many years working with regulars like George Gobel, Charlie Weaver, Karen Valentine, and Paul, got to know them very well. They became like family. Peter noticed the way Paul was with Karen. "I think that he really was in love with her," he said, "but he was Paul. His sexual orientation was elsewhere. He adored her and she adored him." Peter told an interviewer that if Paul was straight, Karen would have been the love of his life.

In Peter's book, *Backstage with the Original Hollywood Squares*, he recalled Karen giving her first party at her new home. Paul was upset that night about the man Karen was dating. Lynde became very intoxicated and fell down, hitting his head on a door. Everyone at the party thought he was dead. They called for an ambulance. Paul survived, but the pain of Karen's newfound love hurt more than the bump on his head.

Paul's popularity from the *Squares* had the press hounding him about whether or not he was given the answers on the show. He most always said they were his.

Paul used the humorous lines the show's writers gave them, and many times, since he did not know the actual question, he laughed at his own jokes when he said them aloud. He occasionally did ad lib, and his off-the-cuff answers were often funnier than the ones provided for him. Like the time Peter asked him, "Who's generally better looking: a fairy or a pixie?"

Paul answered in a very macho voice, with the scripted answer, "Looks aren't everything," which got a good laugh, but then he added on his own, "Oh, I'll go for the fairy," and that fractured everyone.

Peter said it best when he commented once that almost all comedians either write their own material or they have it written for them. It doesn't make it less funny, it's the delivery and timing, and he said no one did that better than Paul.

"What is a good reason for pounding meat?" Peter asked on the show. Paul answered, "Loneliness."

The audience, producers, camera crew, and Peter had reacted with such an explosion of laughter that it took a while before the game could resume. His devilish grin, along with his mischievous delivery of those double entendres left many women fantasizing how much fun he would be outside that box. Mountains of letters piled in from men, women, teens, and children. Paul took them home and read every one of them. He answered as many as he could by sending a photo of himself that he personally signed. He needed those letters with their words of admiration; he said it made him feel loved.

In the 1970s, there was a survey taken, which asked women who would they like to see pose nude. Paul's name was right there near the top of that list. Though he never would, as he had said on *The Celebrity Game* show of the 1960s, another regular on *Squares*, John Davidson, posed near-nude. From that time on, Paul would make snide remarks to him. He told John, after seeing that photo, that he should have been the ambassador of underdeveloped countries. John did not appreciate Paul's comments. He never understood Paul's attitude and his bitterness, but Peter did, and he empathized with Paul. They had both been actors on Broadway and both had extensive careers in entertainment, but the two became best known from a game show. Peter got that.

Paul continued to do movies and guest appearances on TV outside of *The Hollywood Squares*. Paul's unique voice rang out in cartoons as well. He was the voice of the wolf named Mildew in ABC's *Cattanooga Cats*. Though he was not credited in this Hanna-Barbera cartoon, his voice is unmistakable. He also played a neighbor in *Where's Huddles*, and was the voice of the villain as The Hooded Claw in *The Perils of Penelope Pitstop*, which was very popular in the United Kingdom.

The center-square star had just finished 2,500 segments of *The Hollywood Squares* and was making $325,000 a year. "I can't even get three weeks off to have cosmetic surgery," he told *People Magazine*, where he was featured on the cover. He wanted to leave the show, but every time he mentioned it to his friend Leonard Sillman, he warned him not to ever leave it. However, he was starting to feel claustrophobic in that box.

"Paul and Alfred." COURTESY OF PHOTOGRAPHER DAPHNE WELDS NICHOLS

CHAPTER 8

Harry and Alfred

"It's Mae West time." PAUL LYNDE

"I want to buy us the grandest house: one that a picture star would live in," Paul said to his housemate Harry, as they took a drive into the Hollywood Hills in the winter of 1968. The two of them had been living together for the past six years in a very posh rented house on Phyllis Avenue in Los Angeles. The comedic actor was rich now, as he always said he would be. All he had to do was find a home as magnificent as the one in Ohio, where, as a child, he used to pretend he lived.

"I've been to Liberace's house and it looked like fourteen powder rooms," Paul once told his housekeeper. He made an appointment with a realtor and the search began. Paul was not impressed with any of the houses he was shown. What he had in mind was a dramatic home that screamed glamour and that would outdo all the movie star homes in Tinseltown. He was shown several, but nothing appealed to Paul. Then the agent took him up to a regency mansion hidden in the heart of the West Hills of Hollywood. Paul wasn't quite sure about it at first, but became intrigued when the agent explained that this one was once owned by Errol Flynn. Paul studied the enormous structure and saw the three-bedroom, five-bathroom house had potential. They walked up to the fourth story and Paul stepped out on the balcony. When he saw the spectacular view of the Los Angeles skyline, he agreed on its value at $100,000, signed the paperwork, and was in like Flynn.

Harry was just as excited as Paul as he explored each of the seven rooms in the 7,800-square-foot Spanish villa. The first official day in, Paul and Harry climbed the stairs to the top floor of their new address on Cordell Drive. Paul felt like a king as he held onto Harry and they looked down from their fortress on Hollywood's Sunset Strip.

Paul had hired an artist to do an oil painting of his handsome house-mate, and he displayed it prominently in their new home. He had fallen in love with his hazel eyes the minute he picked him up. The moppy haired terrier was smitten too. He was a Dandie Dinmont, originally from Scotland, and Paul proudly named him Harry MacAfee after his character in *Bye Bye Birdie*. The two were inseparable. Harry followed his master from room to room and up and down the stairs. Each morning, they would go out for daily walks. The passing neighbors would greet them and point to the dog and ask, "What breed is that?"

"Shetland pony," Paul cracked.

Happy-go-lucky Harry enjoyed the limousine rides with his owner to and from the television studios. Paul even showcased Harry on *Squares* and on his ABC one-hour specials. This lad also performed in shows. He was a prized show dog who had star status like his master. Paul made sure his furry pal always looked the part of a pedigreed star and spared no expense, even flying him from L.A. to Kansas, for a haircut by the best dog groomer Paul could find.

Paul had practically torn every original piece of material out of this new home. He had already spent more than double what he paid for the place, and he continued to make improvements. He had some big, black New Orleans-style gates put in at the entrance and black iron on the huge windows and balconies. He hired interior decorator J.P. Mathieu, who arranged Paul's expensive French and Venetian antiques (said to be worth $50,000), paintings, and furniture tastefully throughout the mansion. The star had put all his memorabilia, posters, and photos from his performances in one place: one of the two dens, which was painted in all yellow and brown. When Paul was first shown the dining area, he looked up at the mirrored ceiling and thought, "Oh, it's Mae West time," as he told a reporter. He decided it to keep it because it was just flamboyant enough and also made the room look twice its size.

He had dined at a restaurant in New York where the walls were painted red, and he loved it so much that he had his dining room done in the same color. The mirrored ceiling softly echoed the warm, romantic color and the table top caught the ripples of the sparkling water from his swimming pool four floors below. Paul added a crystal chandelier and candle lights, and this became his favorite room in the house.

He couldn't wait to tell all his friends that the great actor Errol Flynn once owned his home. Paul had seen the good-looking romantic swashbuckler in *Captain Blood* back in 1935 and a year later in the *The Charge of the Light Brigade*. Women swooned over him and men admired him. Errol was the top box-office draw at that time and became even more famous when he starred in *The Adventures of Robin Hood*. He had a reputation both on and off the screen as a heavy drinker and a womanizer. The other home he owned he actually lived in; it was known as Mulholland Farm. Paul idolized Errol and thought he was one of the best actors of all time.

Paul had worked with Errol one time, in 1956, on the Martha Raye show. He had admired him and thought of how Errol's drinking and harsh lifestyle led him to an early grave. He had died of a heart attack just three years later — he was only fifty years old. On examination of Errol's body, it was said he had massive coronary disease, sclerosis of the liver, and his insides looked like that of an eighty-year-old man. Paul shuddered, then he called his sister Helen, who lived nearby, and six friends to come for a dinner party to celebrate his new abode.

His friends and family couldn't get over what a dream house Paul had turned the place into. There was a sauna and sunken marble tubs, a fireplace mantel that he had flown in from Italy, and he added skylights. He was always the perfect host and proudly said, "I'm still one of the best waiters in the world." He personally cooked the fabulous dinners that he placed on the candlelit, mirrored table. Paul told *Modern Screen* magazine that the women loved they way they looked in the room's romantic lighting. "When the ladies are happy, the men are happy," Paul wisely stated.

After the last guest went home, the bachelor retired to bed. He awoke to the sounds of telephones ringing, but it wasn't his phone. He stayed up half the night trying to figure out where these phones were that kept ringing. He hired experts to come in during the week to investigate, but they could not find an explanation. It was quiet for weeks, but then those mysterious phones began ringing again.

Ghosts! They were calling Errol, Paul surmised. He told a reporter that, during the first week after moving in, he had discovered an odd little room near the pool. When he opened its door he was baffled by what he found. The room was filled with a switchboard and telephones. He thought Errol had possibly been a bookie but, after some research, learned that the clever lover had never given the same phone number out to any two girls he met. Paul had the room stripped the following month and turned it into a guest room, but was still occasionally hearing phones ringing in the middle of the night. Rock star Rick Nelson and his daughter Tracy also reported strange and haunting happenings after they had moved into Errol's other home, Mulholland Farm. It had become so frightening that Tracy moved out. One late night, when Paul's sleep was interrupted again by those ringing phones, he became so frustrated and thought, *Oh my goodness Errol, that's disgu-u-u-usting!*

After having many parties at his home, Paul decided he would invite, for the first time, Peter Marshall. According to Peter, he was booked for another gig that same night and was unable to attend. When he called the host to apologize, Paul became upset and told Peter that the party was for him. Peter corrected him politely, "No, Paul, the party is for you." Paul never invited him again, but they still got along.

Kaye Ballard was appalled when Paul gave another party and wouldn't let anyone in his house. "We had to eat in the garden." He didn't want it to get messed up. Kaye thought he was being ridiculous. He was well aware he was a neat nut. Once, Jan Forbes picked up an ashtray from Paul's table and he warned her, *"Do-o-o-n-n-n-t* move that." It seemed his home was the only thing he had any control over in his life. He once asked Jan, "What is this castle a substitute for?"

After having entertained the night before, Paul was sunning himself by his pool while his dog roamed the backyard. The phone rang, Paul got up from his lounge chair, and he went into the kitchen where the phone was. He called Harry to come follow him, but the dog ignored him. Paul spoke to his manager for a few minutes and then hung up and went back outside. He called his dog's name again, but Harry did not come to him. He searched his entire property, then all the rooms in his house, and then went through the neighborhood by foot and later by car. He wrote out a description of his dog and offered a reward for his return, then posted the signs throughout the area until it was dark. He waited at home, but no one called, and there was still no sign of his canine. He went to bed, but barely slept.

Early the next morning, the doorbell rang and Paul leaped from his bed, hoping it was someone who had found his buddy. When he opened the door, a disgruntled neighbor handed him a very dirty Harry. He had found the dog devouring his prized roses. Paul gave him the reward and gave Harry a bath.

When Harry was fourteen years old, he had something on his right front paw and needed an operation. His master was nervous that his best friend would not pull through. He took extra good care of him and was relieved when Harry healed. Paul realized he could no longer take his dog with him when he traveled for summer stock; Harry was too old now to be tranquilized for the plane ride. "I wish I had a motor home so I could take Harry with me on the road," Paul told his friends and the media.

In 1971, Paul performed in *Plaza Suite*, a Neil Simon play that had three different stories going on in the same hotel. It was the first time he would be playing a multi-character, and he found it difficult because every other line was his and he could not let up for a second. Wes Osbourne, a radio host in Ohio, had Paul on the show. The star of *Plaza Suite* explained how being so identified as Paul Lynde made it difficult to be someone else. Paul went to see Carol Burnett perform in the same play in Hollywood, and afterwards she told him she had the same challenges. The audience didn't want them to be different from the way they knew them from television. Paul went to school for acting and said, "I always try to give playwright the justice he deserves."

Paul finished his summer tour, which he said was "exhausting, but rewarding," and he returned home. He picked up Harry from the kennel and it was a happy reunion. This time, the fourteen-year-old dog was having trouble getting up the stairs. When he saw his pal struggling, Paul decided it was time to sell his four-story home and buy a one-level property. Before that could happen, Harry became so feeble that his master had to have him put to eternal sleep.

"He was the greatest pal I've ever had in my life. He was as close as a lover, a wife. He was all I had ever wanted anyone to be to me, but no one was," Paul told Betty Garret of *Ohio Magazine*. That night, Paul pulled up in his driveway and got out of the car holding the empty leash. He opened the front door, and the silence in the house got to him. He walked to his bedroom and shut the door. The only sound heard that night was the muffled sound of a grown man's anguish.

Paul immersed himself in work. One day when he was coming home from NBC studios, he told a reporter that he found a note by the front door that read:

If you call the police this will be scandal number one.

His house had been robbed: all his jewelry and silver were gone. Paul immediately picked up his phone and dialed 911. The police investigated and reported that there was no sign of a break in. This added more misery to the already distressed homeowner who had to face the fact that someone he trusted had stolen from him. The very next call he made was to have the most advanced alarm system installed that his money could buy. He wasn't threatened by the blackmail and told a reporter, "There's nothing about me that's not known."

Paul dreaded going home each evening without his little pal there to greet him. His friends suggested he get another dog, but he was certain if he did, Harry would be furious.

Paul went back on the road in July and starred with Elizabeth Allen in *The Impossible Years*. He played Dr. Kingsley, a psychiatrist and father, who was writing a book about raising kids even though his own children were out of control. When he did the show in Wisconsin, *The Milwaukee Sentinel* gave the show an unfavorable review; but when he performed in the picnic state, the *Toledo Blade* raved. The star of the show usually worked his tour so that he could attend his annual high school reunion in Mount Vernon each summer. He would chat with his classmates until the sun came up, and in the afternoon he would join his relatives for a picnic.

While he was in the neighborhood, Paul played meteorologist. He was a guest on television station WSPD-TV in Toledo. He thought it would be easy, since he always followed the weather to plan picnics, but when he couldn't keep up with the monitors, he became even more amusing. He would read the information and think he was done, and then the two news anchors would laugh as they tried to have him follow the prompters that flashed information so quickly he didn't even get a chance to read them. It was sixty-nine degrees in Seattle, Washington, that day, and Paul laughed as he said, "I have a niece who lives there. Well happy sixty-n-i-i-i-ine." When he missed the forecast for boaters, he finally threw his hands up and said, "Oh, screw 'em." He would have been perfect on today's reality shows.

While in town that week, Paul was handed a message that blew his mind and boosted his self-esteem. It was from Lynn Fontanne. She and her husband, Alfred Lunt, were requesting Paul to come for lunch at their farm the next day. Alfred was a huge fan. Well, Paul could not believe it. The Broadway legends, who were considered the most highly acclaimed acting team in American theater, were inviting him to their home.

Both Alfred and Lynn had won Tony awards and Emmys, both had been nominated for an Oscar for their roles in the 1931 film *The Guardsman*. No actor at that time had ever played their character like Alfred: in at least one scene he would turn his back to the audience. He used only his voice and his body to express the character's emotions. Both husband and wife were highly recognized actors, and in 1958, the Lunt-Fontanne Theater was named after the famous couple.

When Paul got over his shock, he rounded up his cast the next after-noon and headed to Ten Chimneys, right outside Milwaukee, in the town of Genesee. The acting couple's estate was breathtaking, and Paul said the Lunts were the best hosts. He felt so honored and said the retired actors gave him one of the most memorable times of his life. "I was so corny I even had my picture taken with them," he admitted.

The visit with the legends sparked such a good feeling in Paul. A few years later, Paul would pay tribute to Alfred. While on tour in Wisconsin, Paul was feeling good and ready for a new companion in his life. There he was — tall, dark, and handsome, and Paul knew he had to have him. The French poodle wagged his tail as he was led out of the store into a limousine. Paul crowned him Alfred Lunt — after his legendary new friend — and the two boarded a plane and headed back to L.A.

Alfred explored his new environment while his master brought his suitcase into his bedroom, stopping in front of the huge portrait of Harry. "I know you understand, ol' pal. I just can't take being alone anymore," he said.

Alfred liked his new home and his master. The two were becoming good friends. The dog was intelligent, obedient, and loyal. He competed in dog shows and won many blue ribbons. Paul took Alfred everywhere he went. When Jan visited, she enjoyed watching her friend spoil his giant poodle. "Alfred loves sweets and limos," Paul told her. The comedic actor found he had the best relationships with dogs because "they don't judge you, they just love you." One time, he told Jan that he and Alfred had just come back from going over his finances with his accountant, and he was told he never had to work again if he didn't want to. "Alfred and I pranced all the way home," he gleamed.

Paul continued to work and continued to complain about the long hours and the stress. "Why do you do it if you don't have to?" Vincent Price, the famous horror actor, once asked him. "You have this great big beautiful home, so why don't you just quit and enjoy it?"

"Because, I have no one to share it with," Paul answered.

One March day, Paul was cooking corned beef and cabbage à la Lynde for his friends. His housekeeper at the time, Tim Noyle, recalled the events of that Irish holiday. Martha Raye and some of Paul's other lady friends were coming over for a St. Patrick's Day celebration. They all came in wearing green, after an afternoon of celebrating. They ate and drank until they all passed out at Paul's place. In the morning, Martha was frantic because she couldn't remember where she had put her dentures the night before. A short while later, the dog came into the room carrying something in his mouth: Alfred had found her teeth!

When Paul came into the guest house where the girls had slept, he greeted them with a sassy "Good afternoon, ladies." They were still lounging about, nursing their hangovers, and they had not dressed for the day yet. Their host pointed to the sign he had displayed there, which read:

To Our Weekend Guests:
Remember when we insist on Sunday, that you stay until Monday,
we don't really mean it…

And he meant it.

Paul attended many celebrities' cocktail parties. There, he mingled with writers, actors, producers, and agents. He was truly the life of the party, but if he learned that he was invited just to make everyone laugh, he would not go. He did keep everyone in stiches, but when someone would ask him how his career was going, that's when he became real serious. He was worried about over exposure on television, and at the same time he was irritated that many people were referring to him as "what's his name."

Now, most of the nation knew his name. Paul also knew having his home in such a prestigious magazine would show how successful he was. He hoped it would get the attention of a Hollywood producer to call him for that one serious role he had been waiting for. "Something with depth, like *The Graduate*." That movie moved him. Dustin Hoffman had played Benjamin, a recent college graduate, who was seduced by Mrs. Robinson, an attractive married older woman. After some time, Benjamin wants to end the loveless affair. He then meets and falls in love with her daughter, Elaine. His confession to Elaine about his taboo relationship with her mother forces Elaine to leave him. When Benjamin learns she is about to get married, he races to stop her. In this dramatic scene, Benjamin finds his way into the church through a second floor, stands above the congregation, and, from a glass wall, he looks down and sees the bride and groom kiss. He bangs on the glass and shrieks, "Elaine!" If Paul had been given that role, he might have wanted to scream, "Marilyn," in that scene.

Paul felt the movie industry looked down on television stars. He also knew he was stereotyped. Offers continued for him to appear on just about every variety show and sitcom on television. He received generous pay for those appearances as a character actor, but it was many hours of hard work. He still dwelled on getting the right part in a movie that could prove his acting ability. Then he would get paid a lot more money without working so many hours, as well as having the prestige that went with actors like Dustin Hoffman and Jimmy Stewart. He had no idea that his fame was climbing rapidly. He was starting to get the star status he had always wanted, but it wasn't because of his acting.

Paul and Harry." Harry was a champion at this dog show. COURTESY OF NANCY
NOCE AND CONNIE RICE

Helen (Paul's sister) and Paul in front of his home on Cordell Drive in
Los Angeles. That house once belonged to Errol Flynn. COURTESY OF NANCY NOCE

CHAPTER 9

Deliver It With Anger

"You can put words in my mouth anytime" PAUL LYNDE

"I've been saying for forty years that Paul could deliver a punch line better than any other comedian, ever," said Les Roberts, former head writer and producer of *The Hollywood Squares*. "From the very beginning, I knew Paul's personality and timing, so we (my other writers Jay Redack and the late Bill Armstrong) wrote joke lines specifically for Paul and worked harder on it than on any other personality. It paid off."

Les had been a comedy writer for *The Andy Griffith Show* and *The Lucy Show*, among others. In 1965, at the age of twenty-nine, Les was working for Peter Quigley Productions for a game show called *The Big Showdown*. It only aired for a few months and was to be replaced by a brand new show, *The Hollywood Squares*. Les remembers exactly the way he was asked about this new show: "Do you wanna hang around on a new show and be a producer, kid?" He wasn't sure at the time what the producer did, but he knew he wanted to do it, and he became the very first producer of *The Hollywood Squares*. He was also head writer and would write the jokes for the celebrity panelists including Paul, Charlie Weaver, Wally Cox, Vincent Price, Rose Marie, and many others.

Les knew what made Paul tick. He used that knowledge when he wrote for Paul on the show:

> His bitterness, with which he had to live and deal with 24/7, is also what made him the best one-line comic ever. In his film roles, especially in *Bye Bye Birdie*, the characters became bitterly funny as well. In fact, ALL comedians were bitter, snarling out their jokes, and if they got mad at you they would inflict the extra-painful death of a thousand cuts. Few were funny offstage; the only two that come to mind are Don Rickles and Jan Murray.

According to Les, Paul never objected to any of the jokes the writers gave him.

> Not during the three years I produced the show. Paul only cared whether the joke got a laugh, but he truly didn't care how raunchy it was. In fact, if you looked carefully, his eyes always danced when he got away with one not usually heard at a church picnic. His humor offstage was generally — well — dirty.

Les explained how they got away with it on the show.

> Then, as now, the common goal of every comedy writer was to get away with as much as possible when writing jokes for a G-rated TV show. Since we knew that Paul's humor was biting, sarcastic, and sometimes even vicious, we tried to get away with as much as possible. Therefore, when we asked Paul, "Is the electrical current in your house AC or DC?" and he answered, "In my house it's both," the censors had no idea of the double meaning. We managed to do this at least once or twice every single week. Another example:
>
> Q: "How many men on a hockey team?"
> Paul: "About half."
>
> I must confess we got away with this writing for Cliff Arquette (Charley Weaver) and Rose Marie as well. I'll stand behind any one of those jokes. I think it made the world recognize Paul Lynde's genius. I think his delivery made viewers more acceptable of gay people, and it managed to turn the tide and make TV more adult. Back then Lucy and Desi were not allowed to use the word "Pregnant." Things are different now. Bill Armstrong, Jay Redack, Merrill Heatter and I wrote every joke Paul ever said on Hollywood Squares — but even after we'd written it, pampered it, kneaded it, teased it, and made it perfect, we would laugh out loud when Paul Lynde did it on the show. There was some unique peculiar thing about him, about his delivery, about his sheer talent, that made us laugh at our own jokes.

It was different though off screen, Les explained:

If you worked "in the business" in Hollywood, there were no secrets. What do you wear to bed, what was your sexual 'type,' what you drink, smoke, eat, or do when you think no one is looking — and we all knew all the answers. We, of course, knew Paul was gay, and Rock Hudson and Jim Nabors and well, it's a long list, but everyone in the business knew it. I was always amazed that 99% of the civilians, the people who just watched and were never personally involved, never thought Paul was gay. I spoke to the people in his Ohio hometown a few years ago, and no one there ever mentioned it, either.

In the 1960s and 1970s, it was not wise to let the entire world know your sexual proclivities, and the more famous Paul became, the more difficult it was for him to swallow that secret. His alcoholism and bitterness made him so completely funny, but quite often he was not funny when he was drinking, but nasty, even close to evil. Even his good friends would turn their back on him for a time and refuse to speak with him or see him because they couldn't face another withering put-down. However, they all came back, as one would have to, because everyone who knew him and appreciated his talent would continue to love and support him. Because of that, though, he spent lonely nights. He came as close to owning up to it when we asked him, "What would happen if you stepped in quicksand?" and he replied, "You'd give my square to Charles Nelson Reilly."

Charles Nelson Reilly was often a panelist on *Squares*. He was a popular guest on many game shows in the 1960s and 1970s. In some ways, Charles and Paul were similar with their bigger-than-life personalities. Both men were actors and comedians. They worked together in *Bye Bye Birdie*. They were both known for their humorous double entendres. Both men were talented, campy, flamboyant, and gay. They had worked with Peter Marshall, the emcee of *Squares*, prior to the game show. Charles and Peter had done a Broadway play together in 1965, called *Skyscraper*. Paul and Peter went all the way back to *New Faces 1952*. Charles admitted he stole a little of Paul's ways, which he said Paul stole from Alice Ghostley. But as much as they may have seemed alike, they were very different people. According to Peter, he and Charles were like brothers. He and Paul respected each other but didn't pal around together. Charles didn't really have any hang-ups and had a long-time relationship. Paul did not have that stability and he was bitter about a lot of things.

While working with Paul, Les and he became good friends.

> Paul was easy for me to work with. He was not the most socia-
> ble person in the world, but he always joined some of the cast
> and crew across the street for dinner during the break between
> shows #2 and #3, and he had a marvelous, if sometimes vitriolic,
> sense of humor. Like most comics, Paul rarely laughed out loud
> at anyone else, but those dinners showed him off as relaxed and
> peaceful." Paul invited Les to his home on occasion. Les remem-
> bered, "It was once owned by Errol Flynn, quite beautiful, up in
> the Hollywood Hills. Paul was a wonderful host, especially earlier
> in the evening."

In the three years that Les worked closely with Paul, he only witnessed
Paul show his love and affection for one special friend. Les described that
relationship like this, "If Paul was the safety officer on The Titanic, the
first lifeboat seat would go to Harry, his dog. Harry was the only thing
in his life I ever saw him grow sentimental about."

As much as Paul displayed his bitterness, it was his intelligence,
wicked wit, and kind side that won over most of his peers, and they
had mutual respect for one another. "We held each other in high regard,"
Les said. "When I asked him to sign a picture for me that I could hang
in my office, he inscribed it: 'To Les — you can put words in my mouth
ANY time.'"

The favorite joke that Les says he ever wrote for Paul — and the one
that is probably the most famous, is:

Q: Why do motorcyclists wear leather jackets?
Paul: Because chiffon wrinkles in the wind.

"I've written for the most famous comics of that era, and I'm STILL
a sucker for a stand-up guy who can make me giggle," Les said, "But
there has never, ever been anyone remotely like Paul Lynde." Les left
Hollywood and today is a bestselling and award winning novelist. "I've
always been very proud to have been associated with Paul Lynde," Les
said. "And here we are, nearly half a century later, and I find myself still
associated with him — and still very proud."

Though Paul was a huge hit on *The Hollywood Squares*, he didn't
find being on a game show very gratifying. However, it was that game
show that was about to get him nominated for an Emmy. That is if he

didn't find himself locked up. Paul was about to face a judge and be humiliated in a packed courthouse, filled with the people he needed the most — his fans.

A scene from *The Paul Lynde Show* with Ann Meara, Jerry Stiller, Elizabeth Allen, and Paul. COURTESY ABC/PHOTOFEST

CHAPTER 10

Kiss and Make-up

When is it a good time to put your pantyhose
in the microwave?
PAUL: When your house in surrounded by police.

"Order in this court!" the judge commanded on a warm Wednesday afternoon in August of 1974. The courtroom was standing room only for the state of Ohio vs. Paul Lynde. The humiliated actor stood grim-faced and frozen in trepidation, before the robed man who held the fate of his career in his hands.

According to *The Toledo Blade* newspaper, a radio show had broadcast that Paul was in trouble with the law. When the celebrity arrived at the municipal courthouse in Perrysburg, Ohio — just 130 miles from Mount Vernon — there were over one hundred fans waiting outside to see America's favorite comedian. Some brought flowers to adorn him with, kids chanted "Uncle Arthur," and many had brought their autograph books and cameras. They held out their pens and roses, as the somber comedian walked past in silence, avoiding all contact as he went through the courthouse door. For the first time ever, Ohio's beloved star ignored the most important people to him in his life: his fans.

Paul had been starring that week in *Mother Is Engaged* — which he also performed in the past as *No Hard Feelings* — in nearby Toledo's playhouse at the time he was arrested. When he wasn't playing center square, he was playing center stage as a Kenley player every summer for the past five years. He had been hired by a man born John Kremchek, who had changed his last name and was now known as John Kenley. John had performed in Vaudeville acts in the 1920s and eventually became a producer. He had a brilliant idea, knowing most of the people in states like Pennsylvania and Ohio would never get the chance to see Broadway shows in New York, he brought Broadway to them. The Kenley players' slogan: "America's Most Exciting Summer Theater." John hired famous actors to star for each show, among them Ethel Merman, Martha Raye, Anita Bryant, Van Johnson, and Frankie Avalon. Paul became the most popular Kenley player in their history, breaking box office records as he performed for 84,000 ticket buyers.

Each summer, the star of *The Hollywood Squares,* and the most visible face on television, was the lead in these plays. It began in 1969, when Paul starred in *The Impossible Years.* The tour began in his home state, with their first stop in Warren, it continued to Dayton and then onto its capital, Columbus. From every corner of Ohio, fellow Buckeyes would travel to see their state's biggest star. It was here where Paul began to get a glimpse of just how much his fellow Ohioans loved him. It mas mid-July and he had become upset when he saw that the show had been scheduled for the twentieth. The star of the show was well aware that "the show must go" as was the rule in show business, however, he thought there should be an exception that week. He just learned Apollo 11 was scheduled to land on the moon, the same night as the show. If that wasn't enough of a reason, the fact that Neil Armstrong, who would be the first man to walk on the moon, was a native of Ohio.

Even Paul, who was intrigued about aircraft, wanted to watch the world event. He mentally prepared himself for a barren auditorium, but when the curtain opened, he looked out at a jam-packed house. Paul was even more astounded when he saw that people were standing along the walls. The ticket buyers were told earlier that it would be standing room only, but they didn't mind — they just wanted to see Paul or, at the very least, hear his voice.

"It's *Hollywood Squares,* that's what fills those seats. And never, never in a thousand years would I have imagined that reaction from appearing on a daytime game show," Paul told David Johnson of *After Dark* magazine. He would stay after every show, up to two hours some nights, posing with hundreds for pictures. He made sure to spell correctly every recipient's name when signing autographs. He answered their questions and joked with the crowds, but he had a way of keeping everyone at arm's length — just like he did with his closest friends — but he was truly sincere when he told his fans how much he appreciated their support, especially in his birth state. He was treated like a king by his fellow Ohioans, who purchased so many tickets that nearly every show had a sign posted "Sold Out." He waited until the last fan faded from his view and the theater emptied. It was then that he would hit the town to celebrate the show's success. This time it would land him in jail.

After a night of drinking, Paul had driven his car to The Riverside apartment complex in Rossford, which was about six miles from the theater in Toledo. The *Toledo Blade* newspaper printed the story the next day. A policeman, who was patrolling the area, approached him to question what he was doing in the parking lot at two-thirty in the morning. Paul began shouting colorful words at the man in uniform. The policeman did not recognize the inebriated actor, who would not explain what he was doing there, so the policeman called for backup. Another officer arrived, but he could not get Paul quieted either, so they had to arrest him. Paul explained on the way to the station that he was angry from an incident he had recently encountered with the Toledo police, but he never elaborated. He spent an hour behind bars and was released, but still had to appear in court.

Paul waited nervously as the judge looked over the charges on that court date. He could hear the loud whispering, and he cringed as he felt hundreds of eyes penetrating the back of his head. Now his favorable reputation would be scalded in his homeland, and he feared that this bad publicity would affect ticket sales. His boss, John, would not be happy. The magistrate studied the actor's face. "How do you plead?" he asked. The buzzing throughout the courtroom hushed.

"No contest, your honor," his lawyer answered for his client. Then the judge slapped his fellow Ohioan with a $100 fine. The charge: public intoxication. The judge also added ten dollars for court fees. The star exited the courtroom in silence and hurried past the adoring crowd. The disenchanted fans' faces fell when the star did not acknowledge even one of them.

That evening, back at the Masonic Auditorium in Toledo, the apprehensive actor went over his lines in the dressing room. It was two minutes to show time and he had prepared himself for lots of vacant seats and, no doubt, harassing hecklers that would come just to tear him to pieces. He held his breath as he walked on stage and was taken aback when thundering applause and cheers surged from a full house. The fans were still there for him. Relief spilled out of him, and he gratefully poured every ounce of it into his performance. When Paul took his final bow for that evening, the adoration from the audience filled the auditorium and the star. His green eyes lit up as he gave a nod for their unconditional love. No hard feelings proved to be true for just about everyone in Ohio on that night.

When Paul returned to Toledo, one year later to perform again at the same theatre, the city welcomed him with open arms, and almost every paper in his home state, as always, gave him rave reviews.

Paul continued as a Kenley player, going on to do *Plaza Suite* in 1971, with Renee Orin, who had starred in *Plain and Fancy* among many other Broadway hits in the past. After each show, Paul told the audience, "Keep laughing always and love each other." He played a father in *My Daughter is Rated X* in 1973, with Elizabeth Allen, who played his wife. Two years later, Paul performed with Alice Ghostley in *Stop Thief Stop*. He enjoyed this type of acting as this is what he went to college for and felt that was the only venue that allowed him to show his acting ability. When someone referred to him as a comedian, Paul quickly corrected them, "I'm an actor-comedian and there's a difference."

In 1974, John Kenley told George Anderson, of the *Pittsburgh Post Gazette,* that the salary of his actors were "astronomical." He said, "Paul Lynde was the highest paid actor in the world." Paul was paid $30,000 a week for summer tours, but took a cut in salary for John.

In between summer tours and *Squares*, Paul became a rat and loved it. Production companies Hanna-Barbera, Sagittarius, and Paramount released the animated hit movie *Charlotte's Web* that year. The cast of voices included Debbie Reynolds as Charlotte the spider, Henry Gibson as Wilbur the pig, Agnes Moorehead as the voice of the goose, and Paul Lynde for the voice of Templeton, the cynical rat. "Templeton is so meeeean," Paul told a reporter, and he loved playing a villain.

Paul also appeared in commercials for Manufacturers Hanover Bank as the nervous customer who is suspicious when all the bank tellers are so pleasant to him.

In 1975, Paul played the voice of *Huggo the Hippo.* The animated film did not do well in the box office, but it did not affect Paul's popularity. The side-splitting zingers that he delivered on *The Hollywood Squares* continued to have its millions of viewers glued to their television sets. They were waiting and hoping that he would be called on, just so they could hear what shocking thing he would say next.

Paul reigned over the television industry that decade, and was showered with awards. According to *California Life* magazine, Paul was rated "America's Favorite Comedian" in the Photoplay Gold Medal Awards poll in 1972. Then, according to the 1978 playbill for *The Impossible Years,* he could hardly believe it when he won "Funniest Man of the Year" in 1975. "I was in total shock," he said on the daytime talk show *Mid-day Live.* Carol Burnett had just won "Funniest Woman of the Year," and when his name was announced, Paul gave her a bear hug on his way to the podium and said he almost crushed Carol Burnett to death. "She's slender and they said her eyes came out of her head. I thought I heard bones crushing." He was up against some of the most talented men television had ever known. Twelve months later, 8,000 members of the American Guild of Variety Artists chose him as "Comedian of the Year." Paul was especially proud of this one because the votes had come from his peers. At last, he was reaping what he had sown so very long ago. He was again honored when the American Academy of Humor voted him Funniest Man in America in 1975. That same year he was ranked fifth in Weekly Variety's "TV Q" popularity poll, in the category of "All male Performers not appearing in a Regular Television Series." However, the trophy Paul still cherished the most came in 1970, from his alma mater, Northwestern University, where he was bestowed the Alumni Association Merit of Achievement Award. It was the highest honor ever given, and he was the only actor to ever receive it.

For two decades prior, Paul was ridden with anxiety about every aspect of his career. He worried he wasn't funny and that his talent was not appreciated. Now he had to add a new concern to his pile. "The more famous I become the harder it is stay on top. You're only as good as your last joke."

Once, he went on *The Mike Douglas Show* carrying a huge book, and the host asked him, "Is that a Bible?"

Paul answered, "No, this is my list of fears."

After Gabe Kaplan had presented Paul with the award for "Best male Comedy Star of the Year," Jackie Gleason, who was also on stage, asked the winner, "How does it feel to be the funniest man of 1975?"

Paul answered, saying he didn't want that kind of pressure. Then he said, "Love is giving and this award is love; and since I am the funniest man of 1975, I have the authority to give it to the funniest man ever." Then he handed his trophy to Mr. Gleason.

Paul had admired and worked with *The Honeymooners* star on *The Jackie Gleason* show in the 1960s, where he played a talent scout. A year later, Gleason told a reporter that Lynde had surprised him with the award, and that he put it down during the show and somehow it got lost. (If Paul knew that, he would have been furious.)

Paul's enduring fame would soon get him the call he had long awaited. Bill Asher was also known as the "The man who invented sitcoms," and he was ready once again, to create a new one — and he wanted Paul to star in it. Bill always said Paul had enormous talent and always felt he should have his own series. Paul was thrilled, but he did not know what kind of show they should do. He told the *Pittsburgh Gazette* that he had called Lucille Ball, and she suggested he do a family show because it had potential to stay on the air for many years. Paul went with her advice and told Bill. Bill thought about *Howie*, a pilot they did ten years ago that never sold. Paul had played a lawyer who lived on Long Island with his wife. They have a brilliant son-in-law who doesn't work and drives his father-in-law crazy when he moves in with them. That show had originally been scheduled to replace the *Dick Van Dyke Show*, which, in the first showing, did not get good ratings, but then it took off and became a long-running hit. Both Bill and Paul thought *Howie* would now have a real chance, so Bill dug out the old script and began tweaking it.

Bill would create, produce, and direct *The Paul Lynde Show*. He kept most of the format from *Howie*. The star of the new show headed to Burbank studios on Olive Street, where the rehearsals with his television family would take place. He starred as Paul Simms, a respected lawyer who was married to Martha, played by his attractive longtime friend Elizabeth Allen. Liz told reporters that Paul was her best friend.

The sitcom was filmed in front of a live audience. Paul and Martha Simms had two daughters, the youngest, Sally, was played by Pamelyn Ferdin and the older daughter, Barbara, was played by Jane Actman. Barbara was married to the genius Howie, played by John Calvin. Jerry Stiller and Anne Meara would make several appearances as Howie's parents. Howie, who has no money and no job, moves into the Simms's home and agitates his father-in-law, Paul, so much that Paul needs a cocktail every night to keep from exploding.

"I'll get you your martini," Martha says to Paul. "How do you want it, straight or on the rocks?"

"Just fast," Paul answered.

Bill filmed the pilot and sent it off. Paul exited the studio and headed to his favorite fast food places in the area: Burger King, Jack-in-the-Box, and Denny's. The next day, he went to the supermarket and bought all his favorite junk food. When he came home he had a feast. "My bed looked like a cafeteria," he told Peggy Hudon of *TV Stars of '73*. He had gained twenty-eight pounds while waiting to hear if the network would air his new show. Then Bill called him with great news: ABC bought a full season. Forty-five-year-old Paul then threw out all the junk food, went on a diet, and began exercising every day. He lost every pound he had put on. The actor immersed himself in the new show that headlined his name.

He had enormous hopes that *The Paul Lynde Show* would stay on the air for years. He told the writers, "Don't write Paul Lynde lines. Write good lines and have Paul Lynde say them."

Earl Wilson, long-time columnist and fan who had once appeared with Paul in *Beach Blanket Bingo* seven years earlier, went to visit him at the studio one afternoon. Earl wrote about it in his column titled: "It Happened Last Night." He had anticipated some good laughs from his old friend, but Paul was very uptight about his new show that day. He was having a hard time getting used to teleprompters and was in a frenzy trying to rewrite some of the lines. While Earl and Paul were talking, someone stopped in and mentioned that they were all sitting in the dressing room that Judy Garland used for *A Star is Born*. "I'll try not to end up like she did," Paul snarled.

At times, *The Paul Lynde Show* was put in the same time slot as the most watched television shows at the time, one of them being *The Carol Burnett Show*. His first show had high Nielsen ratings and Paul said he felt bad about competing with hers. Carol's show was soon moved to Saturday nights at 10 p.m. The ratings began to dip for Paul's show, so it was rescheduled to the same time slot as *The Sonny & Cher Show*. Paul spent his days in agony, rewriting the shows right up until the last minutes before filming.

In one episode, Paul, as the lawyer investigating the Pussy Cat Theater in town, had to watch a porno film. Disguised in sunglasses and a raincoat, he stares at the screen and says, "Oh my gooodness, no wonder they get $7.50."

Paul came into the studio one day, and the stage manager told him Elton John's secretary was on the phone. Paul was a little baffled and took the call. He was being invited to Elton's opening night concert at the Hollywood Bowl. Paul said to his secretary, "I don't know him." The woman on the phone replied, "Well, he sure knows you. When Elton John is in this country he never misses the show."

The Paul Lynde Show ran for twenty-six episodes, beginning in September 1972 through September 1973. ABC had made a decision, and Paul was not happy with it. The network canned it, along with *The Mod Squad* and *The Julie Andrews Hour*. Paul made comments to the press that he felt like he was "ten years too late," referring to the family sitcom format. It was another death for Paul.

Paul never understood how one little device that was set up in one household could represent what 50,000 other households were watching. He had only met one person in his entire life that had the Nielsen ratings system set up in his home. He did not believe it was an accurate way to measure viewers. It made him furious that it was used to decide the fate of a show.

Some critics surmised it was too hard to see Paul as a father — though he stole the show playing one in *Birdie* and had so many roles where he played an exasperated dad. Others thought it was Paul Lynde overkill for an entire show. However, he was nominated that year for a Golden Globe for Best TV Actor — Musical/Comedy. He couldn't understand it. Peter Marshall explained it best when he said, "Paul was like chocolate mousse, you like a taste of it, but you can't have it for the whole meal." Although Peter said he could and certainly many of his fans would agree.

Even though Paul had several failed shows, the television world still wanted him. This was unusual, as most actors with that kind of track record would never be considered for another show. Now he was being asked to help resurrect the falling *Temperatures Rising* show. It was another Asher creation, and Paul was added to costar along with Cleavon Little, who continued as Dr. Jerry Nolan from the original show. It was revised a bit, though Bill Asher believed audiences would not take to this edition of the show either. It was now called *The New Temperatures Rising Show*. Paul, who never said no to work, went full speed ahead, and the producers hoped having Paul in the show would attract more viewers. The former show was set at General hospital in Washington D.C., and the newer show had the same facility, but it was now privately owned by Martha Mercy, played by Sudie Bond. It was run by her tightwad son, played by Paul. Midway, Alice Ghostley came aboard, playing his sister. Paul starred from 1973-1974 as Dr. Mercy. The character was named by him after the hospital he practically grew up in. Bill was right, the ratings were just as poor as the original show, and ABC canceled. Paul would not be the star of this hospital the way he had been with the nuns and nurses at Mercy Hospital in Mount Vernon. He was disappointed again, but also knew it was already a sinking ship when he boarded.

Paul had a nationwide following, and ABC thought of a way to showcase the comic genius. Paul would star in a series of one-hour specials. The first was *The Paul Lynde Comedy Hour*, which aired on November 6, 1975. His guests included Nancy Walker, Rich Little, Jack Albertson, the Osmond Brothers, along with The Captain and Tennille. The show was done in variety style with amusing skits and songs. One contributor to the *Mid-City Daily* wrote it was one of the best variety shows she had seen in a long time and that Paul was quite humorous, but she could have done with a little less of his grimacing.

The seventies were styled in bell bottoms and polyester shirts, and disco music had invaded America. "The Hustle" was the hottest nightclub dance, and while John Travolta was busy filming *Saturday Night Fever, The Paul Lynde Halloween Special* aired in October 1976. The show was filled with witches, a haunted house, skits, rock and roll, disco music, and songs. The slew of big time stars included two famous witches played by Margaret Hamilton, the notorious witch from *The Wizard of Oz,* and Witchipoo, played by Billie Hayes, from *H.R. Pufnstuf.* They granted the host three wishes. One wish was that he wanted to be a trucker with a CB, and in that skit, he and Tim Conway fought over a waitress, played by Pinky Tuscadero, also known as Roz Kelly, Fonzie's girlfriend from the television show *Happy Days.*

Florence Henderson sang "That Old Black Magic" to a disco beat. In another skit, Paul is granted the wish that he be a rich sheik and great lover. Paul is dressed in a white garment and he is pursuing the heiress he has kidnapped, played by Florence. When she won't get romantic with him, he speaks poetic lustful words and becomes totally immersed in himself and says, "Oh! I'm turning myself on."

Florence said she had always enjoyed working with Paul. She loved him in *Birdie,* "The way he attacked, nervous to agitated style, boarding on hysteria. It was like he was going to explode." She had also been a Kenley player, like Paul. She had performed in *Annie Get Your Gun* and *The Sound of Music,* and her shows followed after his antics. According to Florence, Paul was getting into trouble because of his drinking. He was wicked, and he became more wicked when he was drinking. She also worked with him on *Squares.* "He was such a pro, every minute. In between the taping of Squares, the wine was flowing and Paul became looser. Paul was the funniest man I ever saw. [Though] He struggled and was complex, many of his peers thought Paul was not accessible, but he was," Florence explained. "He used his humor as a defense." She worried that he smoked too much and it added to his stress.

Betty White, Billy Barty, Donny and Marie Osmond also joined Paul on his Halloween hour. Paul sang his signature theme song, "Kids" from *Birdie,* and the entire cast danced to Disco Baby, *(Disco Lady),* as Pinky taught "Tall Paul" how to follow her dance steps.

One of the highlights of that show was the rock group KISS. They performed "King of the Night Time World," as their first number. The Kiss fans loved it as it was the band's first appearance on television. For many of their followers who listened to them, it was the first time they would actually see the KISS members in their outlandish costumes and wild makeup. They also performed "Detroit Rock City" and a piano ballad, "Beth," which to date is their highest chart single in the U.S. After they finished a number, Paul walked over to the band members, took a look at the rock group and snickered, "Just what I always wanted, four kisses on the first date." The band members scowled at him. As a result of their appearance on the show, Kiss's fan base grew, and they forever became associated with Halloween. *The Paul Lynde Halloween Special* was released in Oct 2007, on DVD.

KISS member Paul Stanley said in a later interview that Paul Lynde was such a big influence on Gene Simmons that Gene even went on *Squares*. "Everyone in America loved Paul Lynde," he said.

Yet, Paul was lonely.

Susie Lindeberg getting a picture with her idol after Paul performed in *No Hard Feelings.* Susie is such a huge fan, and she has a comprehensive website on Paul: *www.paullynde.info.* COURTESY SUSIE LINDEBERG

CHAPTER 11

Not So Funny, Funnyman

"I've been cursed with shyness all my life." PAUL LYNDE

"I was contemplating death," Paul told Jane Ardmore from *Weight Watcher* magazine. He was referring to his pre-*Bye Bye Birdie* success. He was there to talk about his weight loss and its challenges. He talked about the dark days when he had become a recluse; the more depressed he felt, the more he ate.

Paul often stated that the fact that he came from the potato-salad belt in the midwest had a lot to do with how he ate, along with being raised during the Depression. He knew not to waste anything, especially food. He once said that being so poor was what made him dream of being rich one day. His whole family loved his mother's cooking, but although his brothers put on some weight, they never did the way he piled it on, and none of his sisters were ever overweight.

As an adult, he had tried so many diets and would lose some weight, but gain it all back. He went on the "Olympic Ski Diet," which limited him to 1,000 calories a day. "I can't believe they skied on it, I could barely walk," he joked to reporters. Then he saw Ruth Buzzi who had lost a lot of weight, and he asked her how she did it. Ruth told him she was on the Weight Watchers program. Paul gave it a shot and lost thirty-three pounds in eleven weeks. He went down to 170 pounds.

Weight Watchers magazine put the now slimmer actor on the cover of their December 1975 issue. Paul posed, with a big grin, in a Santa Claus suit, stretching the red pants' waistband way out in front to show how much weight he had lost. The caption read: *How Santa Lost and Found his Waistline.* The actor-comedian stood 5' 11 3/4" tall. He had once weighed 260 pounds, but was now a trim 183 pounds when the photo was taken. "A slender actor is a better actor," he repeatedly said. It seemed to pay off, as he became the most in demand star in television history at that time. He was putting in 180-190 hours a week on the tube and taking in over $500,000 a year. "I'm the highest paid actor in the country," he boasted.

Paul became an expert on food and was known throughout Hollywood as a gourmet cook. Paul learned good meats growing up in his father's store, and he was a pro at cutting up chickens. He also created his own original recipes to keep the weight off: Meat loaf à la Lynde, Chicken for dieters, and Diet waffles. (His recipes appear at the end of the book.) He cooked and served dinners to his friends and his sisters who would come into his pristine kitchen to offer their help to the bachelor. "Get o-u-u-u-ut," Paul would say. He had that kitchen done in all white just so he could see if anything was dirty, and he did not want anyone messing it up. On the wall was a cloth witch that his good friend Alice Ghostley had given him. Alice and her husband, Felice Orlandi, an Italian actor, were frequent guests at Paul's home. After Paul hung the witch on his wall, Alice warned him that he must never take it down or it would be bad luck. The superstitious actor never did.

Paul also enjoyed dining out. His friend, actress Suzanne Pleshette, would keep him up on all the best restaurants in town. If he was home, he loved sandwiches (which he pronounced "sammidges") because he said they didn't mess up his kitchen, and also because he was addicted to miracle whip. "I eat it out of the jar with a spoon," he admitted.

Though the actor's schedule was heavy, he cleared time to attend the Weight Watchers meetings on Monday nights. There he listened to outrageous stories the members shared. One woman said she had such a rough time eating less that her husband made a cage for her head. He would put it on her each morning before he left for work. She did lose weight, but then found she could then fit her hand up into the cage and feed herself — so she gained all the weight back.

Paul listened in amazement as the women talked about sneaky techniques they had used to "feed" their habit: unwrapping a candy bar quietly without waking Hubby and hiding candy in the night table, then eating it in bed after dark. The latter plan backfired one morning when the woman opened the drawer and found the candy she had been eating was covered with ants. When the actor was on tour doing *The Paul Lynde Show*, he told the audience that part of the reason he loved those Weight Watchers meetings was because he met a friend there. He complained to his new friend that he found the worse part of the diet was giving up the "booze," to which she replied, "You mean you're getting by without this?" And she pulled out a marijuana joint. From then on, Paul never missed a meeting, and made sure to save a seat for her every week.

Paul had learned not to be an emotional eater anymore; however, over the years, he had replaced that addiction with drinking. He self-medicated, using alcohol to ease his stress, loneliness, and anxiety. "I've been cursed with shyness all my life," he told Leslie Raddatz of *TV Guide* in 1973. And he told *Boston Globe*, "If I hadn't been a celebrity, I'd probably be an alcoholic."

The nervous actor never ate before a performance, but after the show he would usually dine out. "Weight such as mine is like an allergy, I could go up thirty pounds just by reading the menu," Paul explained. He told Kaye Ballard, "If I knew I was going to die, I would eat biscuits and gravy until I was so big they would have to lower me with a crane to put me in the grave."

The weight loss took years off his appearance. He had always had to play an older person, even in his school plays, but the now-slim forty-nine-year-old looked younger than ever. Out of the fat Santa suit came a very handsome, sexy man. To maintain his new look, he hired Tom McCauley, a life extension expert. Paul began jogging with two rubber suits and two sweat suits on top. "I tried to exercise for a while, but the only change I noticed were lines on my face, from the pain!" Tom sued Paul later for not crediting him with helping to lose the weight. According to the *Milwaukee Journal*, Marilyn Beck wrote that Paul said Tom helped him loose forty-five pounds and even got him to stay off the booze. Paul told Peer J. Oppenheimer of the *Sarasota Herald Tribune*, a publication that had been especially hard on him, "I've been a long time big drinker who's never been exactly famous for handling booze well."

In 1976, Paul's weight went down to 159 pounds and he was honored with a trophy from his Weight Watchers group. After that, he pledged to himself that he would never get up to 200 pounds again — and he never did.

Feeling good about his body and career, the trim actor was open to a relationship. He met Pablo Rodriguez, an artist, who lived in the village in New York. Paul had been staying at the Pierre Hotel, his home away from home, when he met the tall, slim, dark haired, handsome man from Spain. Paul had told his friends he wanted someone to love him for himself, not for the person on television. Pablo had no idea Paul was a celebrity. This may have been the key to what made this the most significant relationship Paul ever had. That and the fact that Pablo didn't speak much English and Paul did not know Spanish might have helped. Pablo lived in New York and Paul would see him when he came east, and Pablo would travel to the west coast other times. He even took Pablo with him on a trip for *The Hollywood Squares*. His cronies noticed how pleasant and happy their friend was when he was with Pablo.

Paul owned a Mercedes 350 sl and a rare Bentley. The Bentley was worth about $40,000 at that time and there were only seventeen of them ever made. JFK had also owned one of them. The outside was black, and it had what he described as a tobacco and brown interior. He had his California license plate personalized to read Pablo on his prized car. Some friends assumed that Paul would leave him that car when he died, but Paul never updated the will that he had drawn up back in 1965. Eventually, his partner's drinking became too much for Pablo, and they parted ways, but remained friends.

Paul's friends felt that his relationship with Pablo was the only one that ever really mattered to him. He had many companions that came in and out of his life, but still never experienced the kind of passion he had always dreamed of. Kaye Ballard remembered another man, after Pablo, whom Paul had a relationship with that lasted a while, but Paul did not feel the same way and ended it. The man was heartbroken.

Paul had told *US Magazine* that he still yearned for the kind of love he had experienced in high school with Marilyn. He still believed there was someone out there for him. He explained that he had to be cautious because he was famous. "You never know if a person loves you for yourself."

Alcohol now had a tighter grip on Paul but, because of his vicious behavior when under the influence, his friends were starting to avoid him. One Sunday morning, after a night out, Paul turned on his television, and his favorite movie, *Wuthering Heights*, was on. It was the scene where Heathcliff, the tortured soul, was hiding in the shadows listening to Cathy, who was unaware of her lover's presence. Paul leaned closer to the TV as she spoke "…he seems to take pleasure in being mean and brutal… and yet he's more myself then I am. Whatever our souls are made of, him and mine are the same…" Paul knew the next line in the movie, and in unison with Cathy said, "I am Heathcliff!"

Paul in his Bentley in front of his home.

CHAPTER 12

I Sure Need You

"I don't know who the hell Paul Lynde is..." PAUL LYNDE

Paul was not aware of it, but he was about to open a closet and let out an eleven-year-old skeleton. He had been staying at the Valley Forge Hotel near the Philadelphia Theater, where the actor would begin his tour of *The Paul Lynde Show*. It was an evening with Paul Lynde, as himself, something he had never done before. He was extremely uneasy about the format. He wrote much of the material himself and hoped it would be entertaining. This would be the first time he would not be able to hide behind a character. He had also always relied on another actor being on stage with him for support.

"I don't know who the hell Paul Lynde is or why he's funny, and I prefer it to be a mystery to me," he said. He told Johnny Carson, the only time he ever appeared as a guest with the King of Late Night TV, that if his show did not do well, he couldn't blame it on the character. He admitted to the host and to the live audience, along with the millions of viewers from home, that he was scared to death of being himself. Part of Paul's appeal for many fans was the way he was so publicly open about his fears and insecurities.

Cliff Jahr, the reporter from the *Village Voice*, arrived at the hotel. He introduced himself and sat down. Paul was nervous; he always dreaded what the media would ask him. If it was about why he never married, he would talk about his high school sweetheart, Marilyn, who had married someone else, and he would say he never got over it. He told Marian Christy of the *Boston Globe* that if he were to marry, it would be the Mediterranean type, and added, "Women with that kind of background know how to make a man feel masculine as they are everlastingly feminine." Other times he had explained he was too much of a workaholic to be married. He confessed to the press that he filled that void with the love from his fans.

Paul lit another cigarette. He had quit smoking for a couple of months, but relapsed. He poured himself another drink as he waited on edge for the questions, always anticipating the day when a reporter would ask him about the nightmare that still haunted him. Cliff soon put the nervous actor at ease and so did the vodka. The interviewer spoke at length with Paul about his life and career. Then, out of nowhere, Paul began talking about what had happened at his hotel in San Francisco a long time ago. "Why did he jump — no, he didn't jump — why did he fall?" Paul said. Paul had never been confronted about that story by the press after the day it happened, and yet he seemed to need to get it out in the open. When Paul finished talking about it, Cliff diplomatically went on with his questions. He asked him who his audience was, and Paul said his following was straight, not gay. "You know gay people killed Judy Garland, but they are not going to kill me."

The Paul Lynde Show opened every night with the star; he always felt an audience should not have to wait to see the main performer. He waited for his cue before stepping up to the round stage. He was nervous, but thought of how different things were now than when he first started out playing nightclubs in the 1950s. He remembered one painful night in which he was bombing at a night club, when Jack Benny, who had been in the audience, came up to him after his act. He told the young comedian that he had talent, but his unique humor would take a while to catch on. He assured him that just as it had happened for him, he too would walk on stage one day, without saying a word, and the audience would immediately start laughing. Those thoughts were interrupted by the music — it was Paul's cue. He took a deep breath and entered the arena. As he walked to the center of the stage, without saying a word, the audience was already laughing.

Paul did a series of humorous monologues and then told the audience he would be back shortly. While he was changing his wardrobe, Mimi Hines and Roz Clark entertained the audience by singing. Paul's everyday wardrobe was full of stylish clothes as he was always a sharp dresser, often accenting his outfit with an ascot around his neck. At one point, the star of the show returned to the stage dressed in his sequined tic-tac-toe jacket of Xs and Os. A recording of Peter Marshal's voice asked questions from *The Hollywood Squares,* and Paul would answer them with his favorite zingers. He introduced Wayland Flowers and his X-rated puppet Madame, who, when asked by Wayland if she smoked after sex, answered, "I don't know, I never looked." Paul had discovered Wayland when he saw his show in a lounge. The lifelike wooden marionette and her master would soon become semi-regulars on *Squares.*

Paul sang "Kids" from *Bye Bye Birdie,* and he allowed the audience to ask him questions. He kept one of his favorite outfits for last: a long flowing caftan. He asked the audience if they liked it. After cheers and claps, he then explained it was good for orgies…food orgies. He ended his show with his heartfelt words, "Until we meet again, you stay happy and keep well, because I sure need you."

Most of the reviews of the show were good. The *Daily News* wrote: "… Paul's reminiscing through *Bye Bye Birdie,* along with giving some of his favorite answers from *Squares* made for an enjoyable evening." The bad reviews were kept out of Paul's sight by his staff, as they knew he would be impossible to console if he saw them.

During this tour, Paul encountered several upsetting incidents. He was at a club with costar Mimi Hineswhen she was burned on the hand by a cigarette. Paul almost always took his leading lady and the cast members out after the show. One newspaper stated that her costar was drunk and burned her. Mimi Hines told another paper that Paul did not burn her, but that a guy in leather who did not want women in the bar, did.

The other upsetting event was witnessed by Cliff, the reporter, who had accepted an invitation from Paul to join him and his costars for a few drinks in town. They had all gone to a few local pubs where mobs of excited fans surrounded the star. Cliff later wrote in his article, "Suddenly, a hefty woman with huge cleavage and a blonde beehive hairdo emerged from the crowd and charged at Paul, 'You son-of-a bitch-you have the nerve to come around here after ripping us off? Saying those things? I'm a transsexual and you're a faggot just like the rest of us.' With that she spat at him."

Paul was so shaken he was ready to quit all show business. The empathetic reporter helped calm the star down. Then Paul resumed with his show, but he would never get over the fact that someone actually spat on him.

Paul felt personally attacked prior to this episode. Buddy Hackett, the comedian known for his brash jokes, was a guest on *The Tonight Show* and told Johnny Carson, along with millions of viewers, that he was on another game show called *Celebrity Sweepstakes.* He said that the show was different from *Squares* because they weren't given the answers. Paul could not believe the nerve Buddy had. He was sure now the viewers would think less of him if they thought all his funny jokes were not off the top of his head. Buddy had actually been the center square before Paul took it permanently. He was a guest panelist on the show for a while, but then was not asked to return.

After the 1950s quiz game scandal, the Federal Communication Commission made it a federal offense for a network to mislead audiences.

The Hollywood Squares had a disclaimer that ran for ten seconds during the show, which read:

> *The areas of questions designed for each celebrity and possible bluff answers are discussed with each celebrity in advance. In the course of their briefing, actual questions and answers may be given or discerned by the celebrity.*

Those words scrolled by so fast that it was almost impossible to read them. The keeper of the center square could ad-lib if necessary, but he never wanted to be in that position. "People think because you're funny, you ad-lib. I'm a script man," he told reporters time and time again.

Yet, Paul was so outrageously funny in person without a script. He really was the funny guy with quick wit that everyone knew from TV. His peers, his friends, and even the reporter who enjoyed a night out with him, all said he was the funniest person they had ever met; but the comedian never believed in himself enough to chance any performance without written material. It wasn't just the words he said or the way he said it that floored audiences; he was also the titan of timing.

Buddy had once stepped on Paul's line during a taping of *The Hollywood Squares* in front of a live audience. A contestant chose Paul, and the emcee, Peter, directed the question to him:

"According to Julia Child, how much is a pinch?"

Before Paul could speak, Buddy yelled out "five dollars," which did get laughs.

Paul looked annoyed, but then waited for silence and said to the audience, "Stick with me now...Just enough to turn her on." He somehow still timed it right and got the bigger laugh.

That year, Dinah Shore paid tribute to Paul on her talk show. She had invited some of his very closest female friends, Charlotte Rae, Maggie Smith, Karen Valentine, and Alice Ghostley to honor him. Paul commented about all the women seated around him and what marvelous friends they were.

Paul explained he did not like being on talk shows as he felt they were so revealing, and even on *Squares* the audience knew when he was in a bad mood. Someone off camera added, "We all know when you're in a bad mood, Paul." The host of the show asked Paul how he met all the girls, and then she asked him what he thought of Karen when he first met her. Paul without hesitation answered, "Immediate love," and added, "I think she has ESP with me."

Dinah had dated Burt Reynolds, who was known as one of the sexiest male celebrities at that time. She told Paul that, in Vegas, the biggest draws were Burt Reynolds and Paul Lynde. Paul grinned, "Sex and fun."

Paul happily told the story of driving home one night after having a few drinks and he happened to be driving on the wrong side of the road when a policeman stopped him. As the policeman walked over to the driver with his ticket book out and pen in hand, Paul rolled down his window and yelled to him, "I'll have a cheeseburger...all the way." According to Paul, the policeman recognized the actor and gave him an escort home. Paul might have used that line more than once — according to Kaye Ballard, she was in the car when Paul was pulled over and also used that line.

Because of all the tickets he had been issued, Paul's car insurance was astronomical. His costars on *Squares* were concerned about safety when he would drink and drive. Eventually, he took Peter's advice and hired a limousine driver for the nights he went out on the town.

The more serious stories of Paul's arrests and drinking never affected his popularity. In a national poll that had asked 1,600 people how they felt about performers not in their own series. Paul came in at the top with Kate Hepburn and Robert Redford. He came in as America's fourth most popular star. He was being seen on just about every popular show and game show there was on TV. He told several reporters that he was making a million dollars a year and could not believe how much more one could make doing television than Broadway plays. Some of the shows on which he appeared on were *The Glen Campbell Goodtime Hour* (three times) *Truth or Consequences, That's Life, Laugh-In, The $10,000 Pyramid*, and even *The Dating Game*. He also was a three-time guest on *The Carol Burnett Show*, which he said was his favorite to do. Paul was too shy to do talk shows, but every now and then he would agree to one. This time he did not seem bashful at all. He would astonish the host and millions of viewers.

CHAPTER 13

My Kind of People

"A room is like a stage, if you see it without lighting, it can be the coldest place in the world." PAUL LYNDE

Seinfeld might have called it a man purse, but when Paul walked out in front of millions of viewers on national television slinging his shoulder bag in the 1970s, it was more than a little shocking to America. This was on *The Merv Griffin Show.* The host asked him why he carried one. Paul nonchalantly answered, "They just don't put enough pockets in men's clothing." He usually carried a script around, and he needed somewhere to put his sunglasses, reading glasses, cigarettes, lighter, checkbook, and pens. He was photographed a few times holding his man purse and never seemed to care.

It seems this celebrity no longer worried about the public knowing who he was. During one of his summer tours, a man called out to Paul, "Why didn't you ever marry?"

The star snickered, "What do you live in a cave!?"

Another time, he was asked by a radio host why he thought so many women loved him. He answered, "Probably because I have no interest in them at all."

Paul was at the height of his career and perhaps the power of having wealth and fame and being fed up with having to hide his personal life, gave him the courage to be himself in public now. He was the only actor to have done such a thing in that era. As the one-line jokes on *Squares* continued to reveal more and more of Paul's sexual orientation, America was let in on one of the best kept secrets in Hollywood. Yet, his sex appeal to women piled up more love letters then anyone at NBC, and they were often accompanied by cookies, cakes, and candy. Paul read every piece of mail and did his best to answer as many as he could, and sometimes he sampled some of the sweets. This man, who never thought of himself as good looking, was considered one of the sexiest men on television. He told a reporter that he never considered himself sexy. He said he had some women fans who would die for him and some who stalked him. One woman parked outside his house with her child, and when Paul ignored her, she wrote to Harvey Korman, complaining that Paul was a terrible person.

One female fan in particular made a connection with her idol. She was a school teacher named Beverly Mitchell. She had bought tickets to see him perform in one of his plays, and as he signed a playbill for her, she asked the star for advice about a subject she knew he was an expert on: battling weight. The former heavyweight gave her suggestions on how to diet more efficiently. She went back to see the show every night that week and they engaged in lengthy conversation afterwards. Beverly soon moved to his home town and named her dog Paula after him. Her new friend would visit her there when he came to see his relatives. She also made a museum in her home of all Paul's memorabilia, and when she told him that she took her second graders on tours there, he said, "Oh those kids are going to be so bored."

Paul was dubbed Mount Vernon's favorite son. His former high school had dedicated a wing in his honor in 1970, and he was featured in "Let's Hear It For Ohio," commercials. Beverly, who was grateful for her friendship with her idol, wanted a sign placed in town for him. The town approved, and the sign was painted and designed by Shirley Fletcher. It read:

MOUNT VERNON, HOME TO PAUL LYNDE.

It was mounted in front of another sign:

DANIEL DECATUR EMMETT, AUTHOR OF DIXIE,
BORN AND BURIED HERE.

Paul was flattered by Beverly's dedication, but he was a little uneasy when he learned that she dug up his foot prints when he came to her house in the snow and put them in the freezer. Beverly eventually lost one hundred pounds and credited her idol for having been her support and inspiration.

Paul appreciated his women fans; he always said they made the best audience because they knew how to laugh, but occasionally he had to hide when he saw them coming. Many women would clutch onto him and wouldn't let go. He said that was why he always had a bodyguard. "Others would not even touch me if it meant my life was at risk," he said. He was invited to the game show *You Don't Say*, hosted by Tom Kennedy. They were taping the show in their Burbank studio when the building began to sway. They were experiencing an earthquake, and there was an announcement for everyone to evacuate. Paul said the studio floor was actually rolling, but he remained in his seat. He wanted to run for it, but he couldn't get the wires from his mike that was around his neck to come off. There was a female contestant beside him who saw him trying to unravel the wires, but she ran out of the studio. Paul finally untangled himself and ran outside. He went over to the contestant who had been seated next to him and asked her why she didn't help him. She told him she was instructed not to touch the stars. He just looked at her and said, "But that doesn't include an earthquake!"

The celebrity did his best to accommodate any fan when they stopped him in the street for an autograph or picture. One day a man spotted him in a restaurant and asked him if he was Paul Lynde.

Paul said, "Yes I am."

The man said, "Oh please wait here, don't move. I have to get my wife."

Paul said he would wait.

The man said, "Please don't go anywhere."

Paul assured him he was not going to move.

The man begged again, "Please, I have to get my wife and bring her over here…she just hates you."

Paul's packed schedule, besides *Squares*, included appearances on shows such as *The Jonathan Winters Show, The Mac Davis Show, I Dream of Jeannie*, and *The Andy Williams Show*. When he could get some time off, Paul headed to Key West, Florida, for his two favorite things: sun and fun. One year, he vacationed there with two good friends, John Young and Richard Perkins. Richard, who was called Dickie by his friends and Sickie by Paul, had originally met Paul at a party in Key West in 1969. It was thrown in Paul's honor by Jimmy Russell and his business partner Peter Pell. Jimmy, who Paul had a relationship with during *New Faces 1952*, had remained good friends with Paul. Jimmy and Peter had recently moved to the Keys and had opened Key West Hand Prints. It became quite successful, and one of their products was the caftan, and they gave one to the guest of honor. Everyone in Key West was wearing them at the time, and Paul loved the ankle length tunic so much, he had them make him several more. He continued to wear them at home, after his show on tours, and right up until the 1980s.

According to Richard, one evening after a day at the beach, Paul suggested the three of them go into town to a notorious biker bar for drinks. Richard and John looked at each other nervously and with much hesitation, but they agreed to accommodate their friend. They drove into town and pulled into the parking lot lined with motorcycles and trucks. As they got out of the car, both Paul's friends quickly took off all their jewelry and put them deep in their pockets. The three well-dressed men walked into the noisy smoke-filled room. It was packed with some burly men in leather jackets and beards. Others wore blue jeans and many had tattoos that lined their beefy arms. They were all drinking and/or shooting pool. Richard and John looked at the crowd, they were both petrified. As they followed Paul deeper into the bar, an eerie quiet filled the room. The games came to a halt, the chatter stopped, the bartender froze, and the men who were sitting on the bar stools stood up. Perkins thought they would surely be killed. All eyes were on the three well-dressed strangers who had just invaded their turf.

Paul looked around the room at all the bikers, and with his piano key teeth, grinned and announced, "You're my kind of people." The crowd instantly recognized that voice and cheered. They welcomed the star and his two buddies. Paul even shot some pool with those guys. Richard and John felt relieved and put their jewelry back on. The patrons were great fun and they loved Paul.

After his vacation, Paul returned to his box back home where America loved him best. He had given up on having his own show after two failed attempts, and he stuck with making guest appearances on television shows, including *The Sandy Duncan Special*. Gene Kelly was one of her guests and the two did a couple of dance numbers. Paul sang Jim Croce's hit song, done Paul Lynde style, "I'm b-a-a-a-ad, b-a-a-a-ad Leroy Brown." He later played a visiting bachelor friend on *Love American Style*, where he overstays his welcome at the newly married couple's home. When he can't find the soap, he helps himself to his friend's wife's pink fluffy bathrobe to wear when he comes out of the shower. "There's a terrific draft," Paul says, "I should never wear chiffon." He was also cast as the voice of Aban-Khan in the animated movie *Hugo the Hippo*. Though it was unsuccessful at the box office, it did not affect his high-in-demand status. He told a reporter he was now making over a million dollars a year.

During the summer break from *Squares*, the popular Kenley player set out on tour again and starred in *Stop Thief Stop*. Alice Ghostly played his ex-wife. Their unique, yet similar, voices had a stereo effect. They had met back in *New Faces 1952*. "People say we sound alike, but Alice is from Oklahoma and I am from Ohio," Paul pointed out. Many thought they were related.

Paul still had some over-the-top zingers. Question: "Is using an electric vibrating machine a good way to lose weight?" Paul's answer: "That's what I told the saleslady, but she just winked." Letters piled in from significant admirers for the belly laughs he produced on *Squares*. Katherine Hepburn wrote to him; so did Greta Garbo. Even former president Harry Truman, who liked to take walks each day, made sure he was back in time for the show, so he wouldn't miss the next outrageous thing Paul would say.

In 1976, *The Donny and Marie* [Osmond] *Show* debuted in 1976. The brother-and-sister act was an hour show filled with singing, dancing, and skits that included famous guests. Paul was a semi-regular, making over thirty guest appearances during the three years the show aired. He performed with Andy Gibb as a scout master; he was a part of a spoof on *Star Wars* where he played an Imperial Officer trying to seize Luke Skywalker, played by Donny; Paul was also a wicked witch called Esther, in a parody of *The Wizard of Oz*, in which Lucille Ball played the Tin Man, Ray Bolger was the Scarecrow, Paul Williams was the cowardly lion and Marie played Dorothy. He helped keep the ratings up for that show. Donny said the best person to learn timing from was Paul.

In the spring of 1977, Paul hosted another one-hour ABC special. His guests included two former attendees from Northwestern: his friend Cloris Leachman, who had been starring in her show at the time, *Phyllis*; and Tony Randall, who was known on his television show as the neat one on *The Odd Couple*. Paul was the only one of the three to graduate from the school, and told the audience, "As a result, they both have their own series while I stand around and watch Donny break balloons." In one of the skits, titled "Bride and Gloom," Paul played the organist for a wedding. The bride, played by Cloris, is his former sweetheart who dumped him for the groom. Paul begins playing "The Wedding March" as the bride begins to walk down the aisle. Suddenly his fingers violently switch to playing "Tramp, Tramp, Tramp." One of the stars from the hit mini-series *Roots*, LeVar Burton, joined the cast. KC and the Sunshine Band performed some of their hit songs, "That's The Way (I Like It)" and "Shake Your Booty."

KC, whose real name is Harry Wayne Casey, had met Paul when they were both at the same management company, and Paul loved his music. KC had also been a panelist on *The Hollywood Squares* a few times. According to KC, he had filled in the middle square one time when Paul became a little too tipsy. He found Paul to be a very kind and generous person who seemed to make time for everyone. He was a big star. KC had done a lot of TV shows back then, and some of the hosts were not so nice, but Paul was one of the rare ones that seemed to have time for him, and KC appreciated that. KC never felt like he fit in the L.A. scene, but Paul reassured him that he didn't have to be a part of it just to be his friend. "I just remember him as a lot of fun and being the person America fell in love with." *Variety* gave Paul and that show a good review.

In his next one-hour special, Paul played a tycoon in one of the skits. "J. Paul Gotrocks here, the richest man in the world," he said, "Get me Bulgaria. No I don't want to call Bulgaria; I want to buy it." Paul helped write some of the sketches for that show, and his guests included Brenda Vaccaro, Harry Morgan, and Juliet Prowse.

About this time, Paul began looking for a smaller one-level home, and he found one in Beverly Hills, but he wanted to have a lot of work done on it. He was at a party at Rock Hudson's house and loved how Rock's home was designed. He asked the host for a recommendation. Rock introduced him to his designer, Reginald Adams, who was also a guest at the party and had just finished working on Jim Nabors's home. Paul and Reginald hit it off. The next week, the interior designer arrived at Paul's new home on North Palm Drive and listened to his client. According to Reginald, he initially thought Paul would be difficult to work with, but he was easy. He just had one request, "I want my home, when people see it, to say 'This is the home of a star!'"

Reginald accomplished that task. The original sliding glass doors were taken out and replaced with arched French ones. Paul had purchased a Chinese screen years earlier, and the interior decorator hung it over Paul's white sofa, which he lined with white and blue pillows. Draperies were hung floor to ceiling, along with brush steel paneling. Paul loved the red color he had in his former dining room so much that he had it duplicated in his new place. He had a Venetian mirrored octagon table that fit perfectly there. He surrounded the mirrored table with eight gold upholstered chairs.

The new homeowner wanted to have the same security system he had in his former home, but this time he wanted to add an emergency button and have it installed in his bedroom. Westclox Alarm Company arrived, and Reginald was there when they connected the panic button on his nightstand, next to his bed. By the time the house was completed, nearly two years later, it looked like a palace; and Reginald and Paul had become good friends. Paul invited him and his mother to many dinner parties. "He was a great host and he had a formula," Reginald said, "He would only have seven guests for dinner at a time and only one other famous person there." It was the same method he used in his Errol Flynn home. (It was also the same number of people Paul had sitting around his table growing up.) Over the decades, other celebrities who sat around his table included Harvey Korman, Maggie Smith, and Jonathan Winters. Friends were very important to Paul. The most important quality he looked for in a true friend was honesty. He also joked that he knew his real friends were the ones he could call to bail him out of jail in the middle of the night. One of the ways he would show his loyalty was having lavish dinner parties. It gave him a chance to dote on his friends with his cooking…until he started realizing he was missing out on half the fun. He would hear his guest in hysterics and then he would leap from the kitchen, with an oven mitt and spoon in his hand, into the dining room area. His next challenge was to try to get someone to stop laughing long enough to tell him what was said. He especially was annoyed when he missed something Jonathan Winters said, so eventually hired a cook.

Reginald was there the night Karen Valentine was the other "star," and he said it was a wonderful evening. Another time, Paul's party had a lot of drinking going on, and the host and a female guest began wrestling, calling each other names. Reginald watched as the two rolled on the floor laughing until they were so exhausted they couldn't get up — so they stayed there all night.

Reginald occasionally joined Paul for nightlife fun. They went to clubs and he noticed that Paul would never go to a restroom by himself. He was apprehensive about fans coming in so he always made sure he had someone he knew to escort him there.

Paul's home, though much smaller, was just as eloquent as his former one and was featured in the May 1981 issue of *Architect's Digest*. He told the reporter, "A room is like a stage, if you see it without lighting, it can be the coldest place in the world." He was proud once again of a home that reflected his success.

In October of 1977, Northwestern University invited Paul to be Grand Marshall of their Homecoming parade. It seemed that everyone in town came out and cheered for him as he rode in a convertible and waved to the crowd. At half time, the band formed a tic-tac-toe shape — à la *The Hollywood Squares* — on the field in his honor. Though the football team lost that day, Paul said he had a wonderful time and enjoyed the warm welcome. After the game, he continued to celebrate.

Later that night, around 11 p.m., Paul became hungry and zigzagged into the Burger King in town with a friend. The patrons recognized him immediately, and they laughed at everything he said. Paul stood in line to place his food order, behind a six-foot-nine-inch African American male. That man knew who Paul was, but Paul did not know who he was. Paul made comments about the help wanted sign and made a few jokes. He mentioned he was scheduled to work with an all-black cast the next day and then added, "Black people are too spoiled." The tall man behind him was not amused.

Paul was getting a few laughs. Then the tall man's order was called, but he did not hear it. Paul made a comment that he did not think the man understood English, hoping to get more laughs. The man muttered a curse under his breath and then Paul made an obscene gesture at him. Paul explained later that he sensed this man was not an admirer. That man turned out to be a professor at Northwestern.

His name was James Pitts and he had graduated from NU in 1966. He was now Associate Professor in the Sociology Department there at the time. The professor was so upset that he wrote down the details of the incident and gave the story to the school's newspaper, *The Daily Northwestern*. In that story, the professor explained that he had some rage pent up from other incidents he had experienced. Many from the school were upset and wanted at least an apology from the alumnus who had just led their parade. Tom Roland, who headed the university, said it was unfortunate, but told a school reporter that he had heard that Paul had been drinking and did not feel he had to apologize.

The story of the verbal altercation at Burger King between Paul and the professor spread through the town. It even made the front page of one Chicago newspaper. Paul finally decided he should make a statement and said, "I apologize sincerely for anything I said, but I was exhausted." Paul later told a reporter that he was not a prejudiced person, but when he drank, he sounded like one. He became annoyed if anyone brought it up to him, and he just wanted to forget about it. He had no idea his behavior would keep him from having anything to do with his beloved Northwestern again.

After his visit, he headed home, aggravated by the whole ordeal. He concentrated on a new project, *'Twas the Night Before Christmas*, his latest one-hour special. His guests included Alice Ghostly, Anne Meara, Anson Williams, and Foster Brooks, and Martha Raye.

The show was set in the late 1800s: though Paul plays a father again, he's not frazzled this time, just seems bitter about life. By the end of the one-hour special, he finds the true meaning of Christmas. In spite of poor reviews, it later recieved an Award of Excellence from the Film Advisory Board. Paul was understandably quite proud of this achievement.

Paul pulled up in his driveway after a day of work, and he was thinking about his plans for his favorite holiday, which was only a few days away. He was pleased that he had finished all his Christmas shopping. He turned the key in his door and, when he walked inside, his mouth dropped. He stared at the empty space where the mountain of 200 gifts that he had personally wrapped in colorful paper and bows for his friends had been. They were gone. His burglar alarm had not gone off. He wondered who would have done this. He was so upset that he waited two days before he called the police. Neither the thief nor the presents were ever discovered. Paul didn't want to disappoint anyone, so he went right back to the stores and purchased another 200 gifts in time for Christmas.

Paul was relaxing at home watching TV one afternoon when he got a call from Kaye Ballard. According to Kaye, she was watching a show that had a scene in which a girl is being warned by her wealthy father that, if she continued to date her pauper boyfriend, he would disinherit her. Well, the girl left and told her boyfriend that she would now be disinherited, but she didn't care; she just wanted to be with him. The boyfriend looked at her and yelled, "Ya big dumb cluck." Kaye was laughing so hard she just had to dial Paul, who happened to be watching the same program. The two of them screamed for days as they called each other, repeating those words as they roared with laughter, "Ya big dumb Cluck."

Paul was a guest on *The Mothers-in-Law*, in which Kaye costarred with Eve Arden. They also went on *The Perry Como Show* together, and Kaye remembered one year at rehearsal that someone was singing the words to the famous song "Maria." This was after the explosion of *West Side Story*. Perry Como, who was usually playing golf most of the time, asked, "What is that? What are you singing?" Paul could not believe Perry had not heard the song and said, "What have you been doing, paddling to and from the golf course? Who hasn't heard of 'Maria?'"

Paul continued to floor audiences with his jokes on *The Hollywood Squares*. Peter asked him, "Can anything bring tears to a chimp's eye?"

Paul answered, "Finding out that Tarzan swings both ways."

Peter asked another question to Paul: "In *The Wizard of Oz,* the Tin man wanted a heart, the Lion wanted courage. What did the Straw Man want?"

Paul answered, "He wanted the Tin Man to notice him."

While America was enjoying that gay humor in a positive way, Anita Bryant was not. The actress and singer who had several Top 40 hits like "Paper Roses," was leading an anti-gay crusade across the United States in 1977, when she learned an ordinance from Miami was going to pass a law that prohibited discrimination based on sexual orientation. Anita had been well-known for her Florida orange juice commercials and was also the spokesperson for that industry. When that law was passed, she spearheaded Save Our Children, the first organized campaign against gays. There was such uproar by the gay community that their supporters boycotted orange juice. Many gay bars took the citrus drink off their shelves, and when someone ordered a Screwdriver — which was vodka and orange juice — they replaced the OJ with apple juice. They named this new drink "The Anita Bryant." The profits from that drink went to gay rights activists to fight against her campaign.

That September, an organization called Save Our Human Rights held a benefit at the Hollywood Bowl. Bette Midler, Richard Pryor, and Lily Tomlin entertained in The Star Spangled Night for Rights. Other singers and actors who came out that night to show their support included Paul Newman, Olivia Newton-John, Helen Reddy, and Robert Blake. Paul did not attend, but he signed the petition, which had signatures from many other celebrities.

Back in 1961, Kaye and Paul had performed in a skit together on *The Perry Como Show*. It was a spoof of the game show *To Tell The Truth*, and Paul played a lady wrestler named Marilyn Fredrickson. Paul was always naturally funny, but when he spoke as if he was this female wrestling champion, the live audience screamed. Years later, Kaye was on the show *Make 'Em Laugh* and said the public knew Paul was gay, but they thought about it in a funny way. She felt that was what they loved about him. She said on that show, "Paul would have loved to come out, and he could have been the first to really score."

"Paul on the Rocks." COURTESY OF PHOTOGRAPHER, DAPHNE WELD NICHOLS

CHAPTER 14

Emmys and Enemies

"I feel like I exposed my soul." PAUL LYNDE

"And now the award for Outstanding Achievement in Television," announced Gabe Kaplan, on May 17, 1979, from the Lincoln Center in New York, "And the Emmy goes to….Mr. Paul Lynde." Paul stepped up to the stage and clutched the six pounds, twelve and a half ounces of copper, nickel, silver, and gold statue of the prized winged lady in his hand and with all his sarcastic venom he spurted, "Have I finally won an award?…. "Yeeeeeeeees!" He had proudly answered his own question with a grin. This was his fourth nomination for an Emmy and though he was thrilled he was the winner, he felt it was long overdue.

Paul celebrated his new prize with his sister Helen and six friends with a dinner party at his home. Jan Forbes flew in for the occasion. She had been in the company with her buddy's big sister over the decades, and it never ceased to amaze her how different the two were. She found Helen to be quite serious and didn't think she had much of a sense of humor. Both Helen and Jan looked forward to the dinner the host was planning to cook: beef stroganoff with vodka. Paul had Jan take a ride with him to an expensive supermarket in Beverly Hills. After collecting the items for the dinner, they went to the checkout counter. When the cashier handed him the bill, he was flabbergasted. It was $110.00! Paul looked at Jan and said, "Ha-ha, for $110 we should have gone out."

He occasionally would order his groceries by phone and, according to housekeeper Tim Noyle, a clerk at the store did not recognize his name and asked him again, "Who is this?"

The offended celebrity answered, "Paul Lynde, the movie star."

Over the decades, Jan would also travel to New York to visit her college buddy when he came at Christmas time. She and her husband, Joel, would join Paul for a visit in his suite at the Pierre, along with other friends he had invited. He liked to attend midnight mass at St. Bartholomew's Episcopalian church on Park Avenue. He would usually have a second Christmas with his relatives and his friends when he returned to the west coast.

Occasionally, Paul would fly to Philadelphia to visit Jan at her home in Pittsburgh. Over the years, he had watched his fellow alumnus' children grow up, and now her daughter, Meredith, was getting married. Paul danced with the bride on that cold December day and returned to the Forbes's home that night. The next day, he packed his things and was heading out the door to catch his plane when Jan told her friend she had some very good news from her daughter. Meredith received word that TWA was going to hire her as a flight attendant. "Now I can get a pass and come out to see you," Jan said excitedly.

Paul looked at her seriously and said, "But Jan, I've already seen you."

Paul took a trip to Key West. He met up with Dick Duane, whom he had first met in New York in the 1950s. Now they mingled with the same circle of friends in the Keys. Paul often frequented Captain Tony's on Greene Street for drinks. It was originally called Sloppy Joes Bar, which Ernest Hemmingway frequented in the mid-1930s. Other famous writers, artists, and celebrities often stopped in there; and the owner would honor them by painting their names on a bar stool. There were stools for Hemingway, JFK, Elizabeth Taylor, Truman Capote, and now there was a stool for Paul. According to Dick, one time Paul had too many drinks and began saying not-so-nice things. Tony had put up with Paul's behavior in the past, but today he had enough. He took out his paintbrush, dipped it in paint, walked over to Paul's bar stool and wiped out his name. Then he escorted him out the door.

Paul was outraged and yelled, "You can't do this! I'm a star!"

In which Tony shouted back, "*Everyone* in Key West is a star."

Another day, Dick and Paul were out with a mutual friend named Tom. Tom always dressed in white: white shirt, white jacket, white pants, and he had even had white hair. Paul was angry at Tom one day and turned to him in the middle of the argument and said, "Look at you, all dressed in white, looking like a big glass of milk. I'll bet your underwear is just filthy!"

According to Dick, no matter what Paul did, he was just so forgivable because he was vulnerable and because he was Paul. He exposed himself and would do anything to make people laugh. He'd make fun, but he was not malicious. He was an entertainer and never let the party die.

Before Paul was handed his Emmy, he had completed two television specials that year. In March, he starred in *Paul Lynde at the Movies*, in which he played a movie critic with guests Vicki Lawrence (Carol Burnett Show), Robert Ulrich, Gary Coleman, and Betty White. According to Betty, Paul was the funniest gay man she ever knew. She enjoyed working with him and said, "He always gave back." The master of ceremonies even had his faithful poodle, Alfred, make an appearance on that show.

That spring, Paul did his fifth and final special, *Paul Lynde Goes M-a-a-ad*.

LEFT: "Lifelong friends." Jan Forbes and Paul. RIGHT: Paul dancing with Jan's daughter, Meredith Shay, at her wedding. COURTESY OF JAN FORBES.

Vicki Lawrence joined him again, and his other guests were Marie Osmond and Charo, whose trade mark expression was "Cuchi-cuchi."

On June 12, 1979, Paul went to work as usual for another taping of *The Hollywood Squares*. When the cameras stopped rolling, he stood up in his center square, lit a Moore's cigarette, walked down the spiral steps, and out the studio doors. He did not let anyone know it, but he had made the decision to finally break out of that box. He quit.

The next day was the start of the summer break for *The Hollywood Squares* show's employees, and Paul had plans to do what he usually did each summer: he starred in a theatrical production. He was heading on the road to perform Woody Allen's play *Don't Drink the Water* at the E. J. Thomas Hall in Akron, Ohio, which he also did back in 1970. When he arrived, he had lunch with friend and columnist Earl Wilson, who had done several interviews with him over the years and was a big fan. The interviewee explained that he was ready for something new. He was an actor and believed that all actors wanted to do movies. He credited *The Hollywood Squares* for all the fame and doors it opened for him and then told the reporter he was leaving the show. Earl wrote that he was shocked and even more amazed that the anchorman of that show for the past nine years was telling *him* before he even told the producers.

Paul had been feeling unusually exhausted and weak since he arrived in Akron. He was meeting his manager for lunch. When his manager took one look at his client, he became alarmed. The actor's face was discolored, and he looked ill. He urged his client to get over to Akron General Medical Center immediately.

Paul never wanted to disappoint his fans, but he had no energy left and knew he had to cancel or he might collapse. The producer called Lou Jacobi to replace the ailing actor. Lou had starred in the original Broadway play, and he arrived in time for the show. Paul hated being in the hospital. "A rich man in the hospital is the same as a rich man in jail and I've been in both," he later said. "You have no friends and no one can help you." The doctor diagnosed the star with hepatitis. He was treated and released with strict orders to take it slow and cut out the booze. He rested another week, then resumed his tour in Detroit, and on to Indianapolis, Atlanta, and Dallas.

Paul was feeling better, although he was a little apprehensive about playing to Georgia's capital. He had never performed there and was flabbergasted when he saw the size of the theatre in Atlanta, "You could play Aida with elephants," he told a few reporters. He thought he and his costars would look like ants on the stage and feared it would not play well, but it did, according to Paul, though one critic wrote negatively about it. The demand was so high to see the show, that two extra nights were added.

Most of the audiences had welcomed the star with great enthusiasm, but some nights the show did not do as well as others. He did not think it was due to his performance because he said his acting did not deviate that much. He knew from the very first lines he spoke how the rest of the play would go. Most of the time, he only had to say a line or two and he would collapse audiences. When there was only a hint of chuckles, he knew the night would be strenuous. Sometimes, he was able to rouse the paying spectators, and if he couldn't, it took everything in him not to shout, "Oh my goodness, is anyone in the audience awake?"

When he reached the city of Dallas, he was overwhelmed by their hospitality. Many Texans were so friendly that they came up to him and invited him out for dinner and drinks. One man took his watch off and put it on Paul's wrist and told him that would be a reminder for what time to be at the party he was throwing for him.

As word got out that Paul had left *The Hollywood Squares*, some newspapers explained his reason for leaving was to do other projects, and some stated it was because he was still recuperating from his bout with hepatitis. Paul actually had recovered and was feeling fine, until he saw the front page of the *National Enquirer:*

SEE PAGE TWO: *Paul Lynde's Drinking Problem.*

He had been shopping in his local supermarket and was at the checkout counter when he saw his name. He grabbed the paper, turned the page, and his jaw dropped. He could not understand where the paper got the information. The article implied he was fired for drinking and being nasty on the show. He was so angry at that paper that he called his lawyer and filed a lawsuit.

Paul took a trip to Florida in January 1980 and, according to Richard Perkins, he and a few friends attended the opening of The Tennessee Williams Fine Arts Theater, where Paul was invited as the visiting celebrity. The streets were filled with search lights, crowds of people, police, and other notables. It looked like a Hollywood premiere. As Richard pulled up in his fancy two-toned-colored luxurious Lincoln, reporters came running over to the car and began snapping his picture. Paul, who was in a car next to Richard, saw what was happening and poked his head out of the window. "No, no, over here!" he yelled, "He's nobody."

Paul loved attention, but some attention he could do without. He had just finished a matinee show in Flint, Michigan, that year, and he was sitting at a table doing his ritual of signing "love and laughter always" and chatting with fans. Paul Barresi, who was one of the cast members, noticed something peculiar about the movements of one of the men in line. The man appeared to be in his early twenties, and he had blonde hair and a thin build. As he was moving up in the line, getting closer to the star, Barresi inched nearer to observe him. He saw that the man was holding tightly to his autograph book and detected a blade-like item in the book. Barresi realized Paul was in danger. As Paul was busy writing, Barresi leaped toward the man and put him in a choke hold, forcing the six-inch steel weapon from his hand. The sharp instrument dropped to the floor. It was a letter opener. The scuffle caused other workers at the theater to surround the perpetrator. They asked the terror-stricken star if he wanted to press charges. He said he did not want the police called, so Barresi physically escorted the man out of the building.

Later that evening, Paul called Barresi "his hero," and from that day on he became his bodyguard and close friend. Besides being an actor, Barresi was a film director, had appeared as a centerfold in *Playgirl*, and was also an exercise trainer. He became Paul's fitness coach as well.

Paul continued with his tour, doing Neil Simon's *Plaza Suite*, and despite that incident, he signed autographs for all the fans and never let on how upset he was. Beverly Sanders, the singer and actress who was also known for being in many television commercials, was his leading lady. He took some friends out for dinner after one of the shows one night and only had one glass of wine.

Paul had only done a few guest appearances since he left *Squares*, and he was worried that the public would forget him. He also knew he deserved more money than the other panelists on *Squares*, and a part of what had fueled Paul to leave the show, after so many threats, was when he learned that the host of the show was making more money than he was. Peter thought the center square deserved more pay.

Paul later explained to a reporter that he quit the show because he was getting tired. He was tired that his acting skills were limited to a game show. The roles he played in his last two movies were similar to the way he was seen on television. In *Rabbit Test*, Billy Crystal played the first man to ever become pregnant, Paul played a doctor, and his nurse was played by Alice Ghostley. (This was Billy Crystal's first theater-release movie.) Some of the other actors in the film included Roddy McDowell and Michael Keaton. It was directed by Joan Rivers, written by Jay Redack and Joan, and produced by Joan's husband, Edgar Rosenberg.

The last movie Paul would ever do, *The Villain*, was a parody of Westerns. Some of the other actors who starred with him were Kirk Douglas, Arnold Schwarzenegger, Ann-Margret, and Foster Brooks. He was again typecast. He played Chief Ner-r-r-vous Elks. Neither film was that big role that Paul had been wishing for.

Despite having a thirty-year career, which was a triumph for any actor, Paul still did not feel satisfied. He also had no one special in his life. He dated, but never seemed to pick the right partner. However, the mail, which never stopped coming, lifted his spirits. His fans continued to tell him to keep making them laugh. Paul agreed that that was what he was meant to do. After a quiet year, he was asked by the producers of *Squares* to come back. He couldn't take not working steadily and agreed, but had a few stipulations. His demands were met and he was given a substantial salary; instead of being paid $750 per day for taping a week's worth of shows, as the other panelist were paid, he was paid $1,500 per day. His new contract also allowed him to take time off if he wanted to do other projects, and he was even given equal billing with the host of the show.

To Paul's surprise, his box had been relocated to the desert, along with the rest of the tic-tac-toe board. The daytime *Squares* had been cancelled after totaling 3,536 episodes, and which Paul believed was due to his leaving. The night time version would be filmed at the Rivera Hotel and Casino in Las Vegas. The very first show back, a female contestant was asked to pick a star. "Paul Smith," she said.

The host of the show looked puzzled and questioned her choice, "Paul Smith?…Oh you mean Paul Lynde," Peter said, as he broke into laughter.

Paul looked disgusted and snarled, "Thanks for the welcome back."

The night time version of *Squares* lasted only one year. The Rivera Hotel did not renew its contract with the show, and the producers decided to end it. Paul, by choice, was not a panelist on the final show, but he did do a walk-on for the audience.

In August of 1981, Paul realized the marriage he had to show business was in trouble. He had decisions to make. He called a few friends then packed a bag for himself and one for Alfred. He headed to Ogunquit, Maine, which was a pretty quiet town — that is until Paul arrived. He was greeted by his good friend Richard Perkins, who lived there. Paul hoped the serene town with its artistic shops and beautiful white sandy beaches would somehow guide him.

Richard and Paul headed to a restaurant in town called The Fan Club. At that time, it was owned by actress Julianne Meade's husband, O. Worsham Rudd, Jr. The popular eatery had a view looking over Perkins Cove and always had a crowd. Paul entered, wearing his dark shades and a hat, followed by his dog on a leash. The waitress brought the pooch his own bowl filled with dog biscuits. On the table where they were seated, was an exposed blaring light bulb that was buzzing with wires surrounding it. Paul took one look at it and said, "Are we going to eat, or operate?"

After dinner, Richard said to his friend, "It must be nice being incognito and no one bothering you."

"Want to change that?" Paul grinned with a bit of mischief in his eyes, "Watch this." He let go of the leash and let his dog run loose through the restaurant. Then he called out, "Alfred." That was all he had to say. The voice was unmistakable. In seconds, he was mobbed for autographs, and he basked in their response.

Each morning, Alfred and his master took a half mile walk around Perkins Cove. Helen Horn, a local, had just been at a party the evening before with Paul, and was talking to two women about it. She was in the photo gallery in town to pick up her portraits. Photographer Daphne Weld Nichols was attending her client, and her business partner, Diane Dalpe, was playing with the kitten they had just adopted when the phone rang. It was a friend who knew Daphne was a fan and whispered into the phone, "Paul Lynde is going to be walking down your street with his dog any minute."

Daphne was so excited and told Diane, who put the kitten down. They ran outside to get a peek at the celebrity. Helen said to the girls, "I'll get him for you." She went outside and greeted the dog, "Hello Alfred," she said ignoring his master.

Paul put his hand on his hip, "My name is Paul," he chuckled.

Then he looked up and noticed a beautiful picture in the window. By now Daphne and Diane had walked outside. From afar he called out, "That's a beautiful painting."

"It's a photograph," Daphne politely corrected him.

The art lover replied, "Oh no, I know a painting when I see one." Daphne explained it was a photo of her daughter that she printed on canvas. He couldn't believe it and hesitated to go closer. He looked nervous about getting trapped if he stopped too long. He couldn't resist, though, and stepped over cautiously to get a closer look. Meanwhile, Alfred spotted the kitten in the studio. He cut loose from Paul, and chased the little feline around the office until she ended up in a planter. Everyone was laughing at the chaos.

Daphne got up her nerve and asked, "Why don't you think of having your picture taken here?"

Paul shook his head, as he got hold of his dog's leash. "I don't have the right clothes and I need a haircut." And off he went.

A few days later, Paul called the photographer and asked for a sitting. He arrived that morning with his hair freshly cut, and he was wearing a red sweatshirt, jeans, and fisherman boots. "I went to LL Bean and I just love this outfit," he explained to the girls. "I want to be myself, and this outfit does it." Daphne and Diane spent the entire morning shooting photos of Paul in the outdoors. Then they took him down to the beach, and by now the whole town knew this celebrity was there and had all lined up to watch the photo session. The photographers took him near the jetty, and their subject climbed the slippery rocks while the treacherous waves crashed behind him. They thought he was very brave as he stood close to the edge; just that morning, a little boy was whisked away at a nearby beach and drowned. The crowd was multiplying, and the photographers asked Paul if he wanted to get away. "No," he said. "These are my public." He graciously greeted the onlookers and posed for pictures with them. Daphne and Diane were so touched by his sensitivity for his fans.

Daphne and Diane headed to the woods, and Paul followed with Alfred. The photographer had a particular shot in mind, and she crammed herself into an outdoor shower. Paul laughed and said he wished he had a camera to take a picture of Daphne trying to take his picture. Daphne was feeling more comfortable and confessed to Paul that when she was growing up she fantasized that he was her father and Maude was her mother. He shook his head and grimaced, "Couldn't you do any better than Maude?"

Then he began to open up to the two ladies. He explained that he was here to get away from plastic Hollywood, and he wasn't sure about his career. He said he had given up drinking alcohol and was trying to get on the right track. He was there to do some soul searching.

Daphne and Diane had him take a seat in a wicker chair with Alfred by his side. They handed him a Cove Cooler — a non-alcoholic drink containing orange juice — to hold in the photo. Paul hesitated; he was concerned his fans would think it had liquor in it. Daphne told him not to worry. Paul said he was thrilled in his outfit and loved that his photograph was taken outdoors. He said his PR shots were so stiff and superficial. After the sun had set and over one hundred pictures had been taken, it was time to end the day. The two girls did not want it to end, and their new friend seemed to feel the same way.

"This is the best photography shoot I ever had," he told them. "I feel like I exposed my soul."

Paul met up with Richard later, and he told him that he was lonely and asked if he knew anyone he could introduce him to. Richard knew someone in town who really wanted to meet Paul. At the end of that week, Richard gave a party at his home for Paul. He also had a belated birthday present waiting for him. "OK Paul, turn around and see your present," Richard said. There, standing in front of the fireplace, was a tall, handsome, sweet-faced young man wearing a white suit. He looked like a model and smiled adoringly at the guest of honor. Paul turned his nose in the air and said, "Forget it."

"What's wrong?" a disappointed Richard asked, "Not your type?"

Paul answered, "I like them right out of prison." The young blonde was crushed.

Paul and Alfred posing at the beach in Ogunquit, Maine. COURTESY OF
PHOTOGRAPHER, DAPHNE WELD NICHOLS

"Paul in Nature." In the woods in Maine for a photo shoot. COURTESY OF
PHOTOGRAPHER, DAPHNE WELD NICHOLS

"You have captured me the way I want to be remembered." COURTESY OF PHOTOGRAPHER, DAPHNE WELD NICHOLS

CHAPTER 15

Remember Paul's Love and Laughter

"You have captured me in the way I want to be remembered" PAUL LYNDE

Throughout his adult life, Paul would cringe when someone said, "Good-bye," and he would quickly tell them, "Don't say good-bye. Just say I'll see you soon." He was afraid of dying before his time, and he dwelled on it. "I hate death. It took three family members away from me in three months." Paul's parents were gone before he ever could prove himself. "One of the biggest regrets is that my parents did not live to see my success," he said. "They would have never believed I would have been an achiever."

At fifty-four years old, Paul surrendered his dream of ever being honored with an Academy Award. Instead, he pursed a new venture and made a decision to buy a Brownstown in the Big Apple. His plan was to live there most of the time and keep his residence on the west coast to fly back to for projects. New York was where his heart had always been. He needed to return to the place that had always made him feel alive. He wanted to open a restaurant and call it East Lynde. He said he had more energy in New York and was always on the go. That is where Kaye Ballard remembers seeing her friend the happiest, when he did *New Faces*. "It was his first taste of success."

Paul had been sober for a while. He used the same willpower he used to stop overeating. Paul no longer drank alcohol for a reason, but he just never went into details of why.

In the fall of 1980, the unemployed actor was asked to look over a script to see if he would be interested in it. He wasn't. He wanted something exciting to do. Then he heard Northwestern University was making plans for a spectacular event to be televised called *The Way We Were*. Over one hundred of its famous alumni, including Cloris Leachman, Patricia Neal, Charlton Heston, Charlotte Rae, and Ann-Margret, would be appearing on the show. Paul was excited and waited for official notification, but never received any. He was sure there had to be some mistake, and then he learned he was deliberately not invited. That incident at which he insulted the professor at Burger King after having a few too many drinks had soured Northwestern's opinion of Paul. He could not believe he wasn't going to be a part of the university's most successful attendees. During his career he had been insulted, spit on, and almost physically attacked, but he never called the newspapers or pressed charges. He thought the entire Northwestern incident had been blown out of proportion. The hurt was significant, but he did not take a drink.

He had also lost his friendship with Kaye. Over the years, they had shared many good times together both inside and outside the industry. They supported each other as they battled their weight issues and had lost and gained many pounds together. When Kaye was starring in the *Mothers-in-Law*, she had lost weight and thought she looked good, but Paul kept telling her that she needed to lose more. He knew his weight loss had made a big difference in his career. He could be frank, like his father was, but, after a few drinks, he could be merciless. Kaye had experienced this firsthand too many times, and she couldn't take it anymore. She stopped socializing with him completely, but she still cared about him.

Paul was now waking up each morning with a clear head. He told some friends he felt more alive than he had in years. He missed working, but now had time to use the pool, keep up his tan, and enjoy his elegant home. When he lost his housekeeper that year, he made a call to the agency he used and asked them to send over a new one for an interview. The agency called a man named Tim Noyle and gave him Paul's address. Tim arrived at the star's residence and rang the doorbell. Paul appeared, took one look at him, and shouted, "The space ship has just landed." Tim was hired for this part-time job at a wage of twenty-two dollars per hour. He received a check each week from Paul's financial manager.

According to Tim, he thought Paul looked like he lived in a jewel box with the way it was lavishly decorated. There were five bathrooms and one bedroom to clean, but they were always immaculate, leaving him little to do. He asked his new employer if he could take Alfred out for runs some days. Paul and Alfred both liked the idea. Tim saw how attached the dog and Paul were and often heard Paul talking to his dog from another room. Alfred would sit by his master and listen attentively.

Paul was a voracious reader and liked to watch television when he was home. As Tim went about cleaning the star's home, he sometimes overheard his employer talking on the phone. Joan Rivers had called to ask her friend what hotel she should stay in while in New York. His recommendation was, of course, The Pierre, where he paid $675 per night for his suite.

One hot afternoon, Tim saw Paul looking out his back door at his formal garden. As they were working, he watched the group of sweaty young men he had hired. Paul opened the door and shouted, "Take off your shirts, I'll pay more."

The doorbell rang, and Paul was handed a large package marked: "Do Not Bend." He carefully opened it, and when he saw the photograph, he was overwhelmed with emotion. He immediately called his new photographer, Daphne, and said, "You have captured me in the way I want to be remembered."

Paul had that photo made into a large portrait, which he hung in his home. Paul had copies made and mailed out as Christmas greetings to his friends and relatives. That Christmas Eve, according to Tim, Paul was to host a dinner for a handful of friends and his sister Helen. He was anxiously preparing his food and running back and forth between the kitchen and dining room, when he was interrupted by the doorbell. Paul panicked. He looked at the clock and became agitated, thinking it was a guest who had arrived early, which is something he frowned upon. He was a wreck, and in a huff he turned on the intercom from his kitchen and yelled, "Who is-s-s-s-s it?" He was answered by voices singing: "We wish you a Merry Christmas" — it was carolers. As much as he loved Christmas music, his perfectionism would not let it interrupt his dinner preparations. Paul frantically yelled to them, "You have to come b-a-a-a-a-ck. I'm too busy."

As the New Year rang in, Paul's phone did not. He had given a New Year's Eve party, even though he never liked that holiday. He thought it conjured up too many heartaches if it was a lousy year, and this year was one of the worst for him. According to Paul Barresi, he was upset about his career being at a standstill. Barresi would be turning thirty-three the following week and he was planning a celebration at his home with ten friends. The day before the party, Barresi's phone rang. It was Paul. He told him he would be coming to his party and had bought him a birthday present from Mr. Guys, a men's clothing store on Rodeo Drive.

Paul Barresi's party started and ended. Paul never showed. Barresi went to bed, but he kept tossing and turning because something did not feel right. He dialed Dean Dittman, a mutual friend of both Pauls, who had been at his party earlier. He told him they should take a ride to Paul's house to make sure he was okay. They arrived around after two in the morning, and as they walked up the driveway on North Palm Drive, the first thing Barresi noticed was the newspaper still lying outside. The house was dark and Alfred was barking nonstop from inside. They rang the doorbell, knocked on Paul's bedroom window, and shouted his name. When Paul did not answer, Barresi became so worried that he decided to break in through the side door. This triggered the security alarms. He and Dean stumbled through the darkness. Barresi found the master bedroom and felt around for the light switch. When the light came on, their hearts sank. Paul, dressed in his pajamas and bathrobe, was lying on his bed. It was evident to Barresi that Paul had tried to reach for the panic button next to the bed, but never made it. Alfred was confused and terrified, but relieved somebody had come to his master.

Paul died alone, so an autopsy was performed. According to the newspapers, the police records showed two bottles of butyl nitrate were found on his bed stand. One was unopened, the other nearly full. A small trace of the over-the-counter substance was found in his system, but the doctor did not believe it was enough to kill him. The coroner listed the fifty-five year old actor's death as a heart attack. After the autoposy report came in, Paul's doctor told Jan that her friend had the heart of an eighty-five year old man.

The police found no foul play in the actor-comedian's death. Tim, the housekeeper, was asked to stay at Paul's house to keep an eye on the place. He walked around the empty house. It was strange to be there with Paul gone, and not even Alfred was there to greet him. According to Tim, the master bath, which Paul never used and only reserved for guests (as he never wanted to mess it up) looked untouched. Tim felt a need to talk to someone, but felt bad that there was no significant person in Paul's life he could call. "No close friend that he talked to every day," he said.

There were two services held. One was at the Westwood Village Memorial Chapel, in Los Angeles, California. There friends, family, relatives, and his peers, totaling over 250, attended to pay their respects to the great artist. He was cremated. Then there was another service held in Mount Vernon, where another large crowd gathered again, including some fans. It took place on a Sunday afternoon, at the church he attended as a boy: St. Paul's. His ashes are buried at the Amity Cemetery, in Knox County, Ohio, alongside his parents and two brothers. Paul was born in 1926; however, his headstone mistakenly reads 1927. He relatives do not know why.

Alfred went to Paul's niece Nancy, where the poodle lived a long, good life and had her children to play with. Helen, his sister, was so distraught over her brother's death that she hired someone to help with all his antiques, paintings, and belongings. Paul's nieces donated his memorabilia to the Knox County Historical Society's Museum in Mount Vernon, Ohio, and is still on display there today.

Kaye Ballard was furious with him for drinking so much and said he didn't need to die. He knew his father had died young. She had cared very much for her friend. She thought he had such an innately keen sense of humor; however, he was unhappy and complicated. "He never believed." According to Kaye, part of his unhappiness was that he didn't get into quality movies, and that was his heartbreak. Although Paul had done many movies and some of them did very well, he would just say, "I did eleven bad ones."

Cloris Leachman was heartbroken at the news of the death of her very good college friend. She had been at his home recently and had a wonderful time. She was amazed at his relationship with his poodle and got a kick out of the fact he had mirrored floors in his guest bathroom. "Paul was the most original brilliant man I've ever known," she told columnist Shirley Edner. She did not see her friend as bitter, and she added, "He couldn't use his excellence and that itself was kind of death."

Richard Perkins was shocked by the news. He had just recently made plans with Paul to come out to his home for a visit. Richard would be bringing a friend who wanted to meet Eve Arden. When Richard mentioned this to Paul, he said Eve was his neighbor, and he would have a dinner party and make sure she was there.

Meredith Asher, Bill's wife, remembered how Bill adored Paul. She occasionally still runs into Jack Jones, singer of *The Love Boat* show's theme song and Grammy award winner. He still brings up to her that one of the funniest nights, and the most laughs he ever had, had been with Paul and Bill. Meredith has a picture of Paul "drunk as a skunk," where he fell on top of Bill and they were both laughing.

Reginald Adams had the flu when he heard of his good friend's passing, and the stress of the news made him sicker. He thought about the alarm on Paul's nightstand that was installed while he was working on his home. It was so close to his bed where he was found.

Paul Barresi slowly unwrapped the silver paper that covered his birthday gift. It was a blue cashmere pullover sweater, from Mr. Guys, that Paul had picked out for him.

Charlotte Rae was filming an episode of *The Facts of Life* when she heard the news. She and several of Paul's closest friends gathered at Alice Ghostley's home after the funeral. To this day, she says she will never forget those skits she did with Paul during their four years at college together when they were known as Lubotsky and Lynde, or his naughty wit. "There will never be anyone as brilliant or as incredibly talented as Paul was," Charlotte said.

His peers, friends, and so many felt the same way. Dick Van Dyke once said, "Paul was one of the five most inherently funny guys in the country."

"He never had a clue what a big star he was," Peter Marshall said. He had recently bumped into Paul at the airport, and he thought Paul looked great. They had a pleasant conversation. *The Hollywood Squares* family felt deep sadness. Rose Marie lost her buddy.

Jan heard the news in her car on the radio: she lost her best friend. She keeps his Emmy Award on her mantel of her home, and she treasures the box full of letters he wrote to her. So many people who had worked with Paul in the business, along with millions of fans, felt the loss of a great artist.

According to archivist Kevin B. Leonard, Northwestern University is hoping to collect Paul's papers: his business and professional records, scrapbooks, photographs, and clippings.

Long before all of this, a little boy from Ohio found a gift within himself and he was generous enough to use it. He made us laugh until our sides ached. On January 10, 1982, the world lost the most original comedian and actor there ever was, or ever will be…And, as Paul would say, *"That's* disg-u-u-u-sting."

Though it was an emotionally exhausting week,
Paul still smiled for his fans. Toronto, Canada, August 1981.

Epilogue

The last time I saw Paul was in August of 1980, with my friend, Debbie Braun. We went to see him perform in *Plaza Suite* in Toronto, Canada. Paul took us out to a Chinese restaurant after the show. It was Debbie's first time meeting him, and she was so nervous and kept thanking him profusely for his hospitality. Paul kept trying to reassure her saying, "Calm down. It's all right."

The waiter brought over a tray with a dead fish that was over a foot long, and he placed it on our table. It had two huge eyes that were bulging out at us. Debbie and I freaked, so Paul took his fork and stuck it right in the eyeballs. "Now you'll stop staring," he joked.

After dinner, we returned to his hotel, and Paul became very quiet as he sat sipping a diet soda while Debbie and I played with his dog, Alfred. He wasn't drinking, but I was, and when I went over to pour myself another drink, Paul gave me a disapproving look.

Later, when I was heading out, I handed Paul a brochure from the play and asked him to sign it. He said, "Cathy, you don't need my autograph. You have it. We are beyond that." I insisted. He seemed annoyed, but signed it anyway. I did not know how to tell him that I needed his words to hold onto until I would see him again. When it was time to go, I mistakenly said, "Good-bye," and Paul quickly said, "Please don't say that. Just say I'll see you soon." That would be the last time I saw him. Paul died in January.

When I was seventeen, my prayers were answered when I found Paul's phone number. I think now it was because God knew we needed each other.

At our first meeting, Paul asked me what I wanted to be when I grew up, and I said "an author." Later, I wrote to Paul, thanking him for letting me into his life and that I hoped one day I could do something for him. Well Paul, I hope you like it.

Paul can still be seen on reruns of *Bewitched*, as well as in many movies. His voice is imitated by Michael Airington, as the talking mirror on Disney's *The Suite Life on Deck*. Michael also performed as Paul for years in Hollywood in his show *Oh My Goodness…It's Paul Lynde,* and he is planning to bring the show back soon.

Seth MacFarlane told an audience that Paul was the inspiration for the voice of Roger the Alien on *American Dad*. His jokes from *The Hollywood Squares* are still passed around on the Internet. Not too long ago, Ellen DeGeneres, in honor of Paul, held his picture when she sat in the center square on the newer *Hollywood Squares.*

Maybe soon, some wise network will bring *The Paul Lynde Show* back on television.

For more Paul, please visit the author's website: *www.paullyndeabiography.com*

"The Last Time I saw Paul." Cathy (Fitzgibbon) Rudolph, Paul, and Debbie Braun in Toronto, Canada (August 31, 1980). COURTESY OF MAUREEN STOCKBERGER

Paul's Performances

BROADWAY PLAYS
New Faces 1952
Bye, Bye, Birdie 1960
New Faces 1956 (written and directed only)

SUMMER STOCK
Visit To A Small Planet
Panama Hattie
The Impossible Years
Don't Drink the Water

Plaza Suite
My Daughter's Rated X
Mother is Engaged
Stop, Thief, Stop!

TELEVISION
Bewitched
Bob Hope Chrysler Theater
Hollywood Palace
Dean Martin and The Golddiggers
The Dean Martin Celebrity Roast
The Red Buttons Show
The Jackie Gleason Show
Ed Sullivan Show
Burke's Law
The Jack Paar Show
Colgate Comedy Hour
The Jack Benny Show
Hollywood Palace
Smother's Brothers
Gypsy Rose Lee Show
The Farmer's Daughter
The Dean Martin Show

Dean Martin Presents
   the Gold Diggers
The Jonathan Winters Show
The Steve Allen Show
Beverly Hillbillies
Jerry Lewis
The Tonight Show
Bob Hope Chrysler Theatre
Kraft Music Hall
F-Troop
The Flying Nun
The Glen Campbell Goodtime Hour
The Paul Lynde Show
The Dinah Shore Show
I've Got A Secret
That Girl
Donny and Marie

The Mac Davis Show
The Martha Raye Show
The Andy Williams Show
The Arthur Godfrey Show
The Patty Duke Show
Henry Fonda and Family
Grindl
Celebrity Game
Hallmark Hall of Fame
The Munsters
The Mike Douglas Show
The Pierre Berton Show
The Merv Griffin Show
The Hollywood Squares
The Dating Game
Truth or Consequences
I Dream of Jeanie
Art Linkletter

That's Life
The Mothers-In-Law
Where's Huddles?
Laugh-In
Gidget Grows Up
Gidget Gets Married
The New Temperatures Rising Show
The $10,000 Dollar Pyramid
Ruggles of Red Gap
Love, American Style
The Paul Lynde Special
Paul Lynde at the Movies
The Paul Lynde Comedy Hour
The Paul Lynde Halloween Special
Paul Lynde Goes Maaad
The Paul Lynde Show
The Phil Silvers Show
The Perils of Penelope Pittstop

FEATURE FILMS
New Faces 1952
Bye, Bye, Birdie
Under the Yum Yum Tree
Return To The Land of Oz
Son of Flubber
Beach Blanket Bingo
For Those Who Think Young
Send Me No Flowers

The Glass Bottom Boat
How Sweet It Is
Charlotte's Web
Hugo the Hippo
Rabbit Test
The Villain

Paul Lynde's Recipes

PAUL LYNDE'S DIET WAFFLES
1 egg white
3/8 cup cake flour
1 tsp. baking powder
3/8 cup skim milk
1/8 tsp. salt

Beat egg white until stiff. In a blender, combine milk, flour and salt. Add baking powder and beat until smooth. Pour batter in a bowl and gently fold egg white into it. Cook until crisp in a pre-heated waffle iron. (Cook a little longer than regular waffles.)

This makes 3 waffles of 50 calories each.

PAUL LYNDE'S DIET CHICKEN
1 chicken, cut up and skinned
Tomato juice
Celery
Green peppers
All beef cocktail franks, drained
Frozen shrimp (shelled)

Place chicken in a heavy pan and cover with ½ tomato juice and ½ water. Simmer ½ hour.

Chop the green peppers (2 or 3) and the celery (practically the whole bunch).

Add to the chicken at the end of the ½ hour, and simmer another ½ hour. During last three minutes of cooking, add the shrimp.

DIET MEAT LOAF À LA LYNDE
2 lbs. super lean ground beef
2 egg yolks
1 cup canned okra
Salt and pepper to taste
Oregano and/or celery seed as desired
(for every pound of ground beef add egg yolk)

Pre-heat oven to 350 degrees

Mix ingredients together and place in a loaf pan. Glaze lightly with ketchup. Bake at 350 degrees for 1 hour.

PAUL LYNDE'S BEEF STEW
3 lbs. stew meat
1 No. 2 can diced carrots
1 No. 2 can small onions
1 No. 2 can tomatoes
1 No. 2 can tiny peas
1 No. 2 can potatoes
1 No. 2 can small green beans (reg. cut)
½ can beef consommé
4 tbs. minute tapioca
1 tbs. brown sugar
½ cup prepared bread crumbs
1 bay leaf
½ cup white wine
1 ½ tbs. salt, pepper (to taste)

Pre heat oven to 250 degrees.

Blend all ingredients together. Bake in covered casserole 6-7 hours.

Acknowledgements

My supportive, loving sisters: Tricia Pugliesi, Maureen Stockberger, and Eileen Ruggerio. My first editors: Jocelyn Conte and Haley Rudolph. My computer experts: Joan Seaman and Ryan Rudolph. My first readers and support system: Jerry Fitzgibbon, Margo Wieland, Pam Morrow, Barbara Brinkerhoff, Tom Philbin, Arleen Kanea, Bob Feuchter and E. Earle Rudolph. My other friends and family who are supporters: Ana Dolne and daughters Sandra, Cynthia, Patty and Lisabelle, Janet and Lauren Fine, Arlene Duggan, Jean Cutsail, Robin Aaron, Olive Bourne, Amy and Tom Fowler, Susan Drost, Donna Mabanta, Nancy Smith, Lea Tyrell, Claudia Kwasnik-Picarello, Mary Devine, The Callighan Clan, Jim and Anne Rudolph, Kelly Small, Rachel Dannenberg and Michael Cohen, Glenn, Barbara, Jaimie and Gavin Rudolph, Patty Reed, Debbie Braun, The Cecora Clan, The Bochicchio Clan, The Burkes and Hemphills, Lisa Tarantino, Joanne Verderosa, Frank and Cheryl Raffele. The Levittown Public Library, The Comsewogue Library Staff, Sino, Gabrielle and Michelle Pugliesi, Brittany, Melissa, and Amanda Stockberger, Dolores Santiago, Eileen Korpi, and Dorothy Heifi.

Also to Father Bill Hanson who was a constant reminder to use the talents God gave us. And to Oprah, who made an impact when she said to do what you want before you're fifty years old. To Belle, my faithful dog, who sat beside me while I wrote the book.

Special thanks to Connie Rice and Nancy Noce, Jim Gibson of Knox County Historical Society, Reginald Adams, Daphne Welds Nichols and Diane Dalpe, Michael Airington, and Susie Lindeberg. Northwestern University and archivist Kevin B. Leonard, George Englund, Jr., Jan Forbes, Cloris Leachman, Kaye Ballard, Chita Rivera, and to Les Roberts for his history with Paul and giving me the jokes he wrote for Paul from *Squares*. Also to Peter Marshall for his kind help and time he gave me for the book. And to all Paul's friends whose memories of Paul helped us to really get to know him.

And to all the staff at Bear Manor, including Michelle and my editor, Wendy, Sandy, Brian Pearce for all his professionalism and hard work, and especially to Ben Ohmart for giving me the chance to tell Paul's story and making another dream come true.

In loving memory of my beautiful mom, Patricia Fitzgibbon.

Bibliography

"A Practical Joke...then Man Falls to Death." *St. Petersburg Times,* July 19, 1965: 9A.

Adams, Reginald. Telephone Interview. March 2013.

Anderson, George, " Kenley Star Policy Costly But Successful," June 19, 1974: 10.

Andres, Bart, "Paul Lynde." *TV Star Parade.* January 1967: 65, 66.

Archive of American Television: William Asher. Five Paths, Web. *http://www.emmytvlegends.org/interviews/people/william-asher.* October 29, 2012.

Ardmore, Jane. "The Day Santa Lost & Found His Waistline." *Weight Watchers Magazine,* December, 1975: 23, 60, 63.

Asher, Meredith. Telephone Interview. November 29, 2011.

Atkinson, Brooks, "At The Theater." *New York Times*, May 17, 1952: 23.

Ballard, Kaye. Telephone Interview. November 4, 2011.

Barbra Streisand won a Grammy and a husband, all it the same year, *The Milwaukee Journal,* October 28, 1981: 4.

Barresi, Paul. Email Interview. February 11, 24, 2011. Telephone Interview February 8, 16, 2011.

Barts, Andrew. *TV Talk Radio.* February, 1973: 32.

Beck, Marylin, "Paul Lynde has Heavy Legal Problems." *Milwaukee Journal.* July 15,1977: 3.

"Black Professor Raps Paul Lynde." *The Tuscaloosa News*, October 30, 1977: 9A.

Bregman, Buddy. Telephone Interview. April 10, 2011 and Email Interview. May 12, 2011.

Bryant, Anita. *Wikepedia.* June 21, 2012.

Bye Bye Birdie (Musical). *Wikipedia* May 14, 2011.

Casey, Harry Wayne, "KC." Email interview. November 15, 17, 2011.

Church, Glenn, Bottom of the Deck...Lubotsky...Lynde" *Daily Northwestern, Evanston, ILL.* April 16, 1947.

_____ "Kampus Keyhole." *Daily Northwestern*, April 1, 1947: 5.

Christy, Marion, "Lynde on a Little Fling." *Boston Globe*, April 13, 1975: B-12.

Clary, Robert. Email Interview. September 19, 2011.

Cohn, Al. "The LI Interview: Paul Lynde." *Newsday.* October 12, 1980: 25-56.

Dalpe, Diane. Telephone Interview. September 9, 2011.

Dinah and Friends, CBS. Television. Aired December 20. 1976.

Duane, Dick. Telephone Interview. November, 2012.

Edner, Shirley. "Paul Lynde: A Brilliant Comic — cut down at a crossroad." *Detroit Free Press,* January 16, 1981.

Forbes, Jan. March 20, May 12, December 22, 2011.

Gallen, Ira, H. TVDAYS. "Celebrity Game Show with Bert Parks. Zsa Zsa Gabor, Paul Lynde…" *YouTube.* February 18, 2011. Online video clip, *http://www.youtube.com/ watch?v=LQAqt1dQXko.* April 20, 2012.

Garret, Betty. "Funny Man." *Ohio Magazine.* December, 1978: 35-45.

Gauer, Jack. "Two Hits Rescue Theater Section." *Pittsburgh Press*, April 15, 1960: 9.

Gautier, Dick. Email Interview. July 26, 2011.

Hale, Lee and Neely, Richard. *Backstage at the Dean Martin Show.* Taylor Publishing, Texas, 2000: 96, 101, 159.

Haber, Joyce, "Ohio, Cult, Other Unusual Fans Worship Paul Lynde," *Sarastoa Journal,* January 16, 1973: 6-b

Hayes, Dixon. Classic Squares. *The Classic Hollywood Squares.* Web. *Classicsquares.com.* December 4, 2011.

Henderson, Florence. Telephone Interview. May 10, 2012.

Hollywood Squares. *Wikipedia.* March 5, 2012.

Hudson, Peggy. "Laughs are what it's all about: The Paul Lynde Show." *TV Stars of '73.* 1973: 39-47.

Jahr, Cliff, "What's Eating TV's Top Banana?" July 5, 1976, *Village Voice:* 116.

Johnson, David. "Now Let's Hear it For Paul Lynde." *After Dark*, November 1972: 52, 53.

Kasler, Dale. "Lynde Apologizes to Pitts over Homecoming Remarks." *Daily Northwestern,* Vol. 98, No. 29. Evanston, Ill, November 1, 1977:1.

Kayeballarddot.com. "Kaye Ballard on Paul Lynde."

PBS Documentary. The Funny Business of America. YouTube. November 18, 2009. On line video clip. April 15, 2013.

Kenly, John, *Wikipedia.* August 7, 2011.

Lakeland Ledger, "Paul Lynde Loves his Ratty Role." November 28, 1976: 45.

Leachman, Cloris with Englund, George. *Cloris,* Kensington Books: 2009: 34, 48, 63.

Leonard, Kevin. Email Interview. February 11, 2013.

Lindeberg, Susie. *Paul Lynde Remembered.* Web. *www.paullynde.info.* April, May, June, 2012.

Leachman, Cloris. Telephone Interview. January 20, 2011.

"Lynde Rites Set Thursday," *Williamson Daily News,* January 13, 1982: 13.

Marshall, Peter. Telephone Interview. January 6, 2011.

Marshall, Peter, and Armstong, Adrianne. *Backstage at the Original Hollywood Squares.* Rutlege Hill Press, Tennesse. 2002: 50, 147-148

Martion, Alison. The Paul Lynde Story. *E! Mysteries and Scandals.* Produced by Alison Martino. YouTube. July 14, 2011. Season 3, episode 37. Video clip. March 3, 2011.

"Mays Magic Scores on "Bewitched" Set. *New York Amsterdam News.* 1962-1993: October 29, 1966: 14.

Metrolibrarian. *"Public Transportation: Who Needs It?"* You Tube. Southern California Rapid Transit District (RTD), 1968. September 25, 2008. Video clip. January 10, 2011.

Masak, Ron. Email Interview. September 26, 2011.

Midday Live. Television.WNEW-TV Aired December, 1977.

Morrow, Susan Stark. "An Actor's Aspirations Realized." *Architect Digest.* May 1981: 159-161.

Nass, Herbert E, *Wills of the Rich and Famous,* New York, Grammercy. 2000: 215.

"Nervous Nellie of the Networks." *TV Guide.* July 13, 1963: 16, 17.

Nery Margret, "Once rejected, Paul Lynde Wants Love," *Youngstown Vindicator,* March 3, 1978: p 26.

Nicholson, Jacquelyn, "Cooking With A Star, Comedy and Cuisine in the Kitchen." *Bon Apetit.* June 1978.

Noce, Nancy. Telephone Interview. January 19, 2011.

Noyle, Tim. Telephone Interview. March 20, 2010, September 1, 2011.

"Off Center." A&E Biography: Paul Lynde, 2001. A&E Television Networks.Video.

Oppenheimer, Peer J. "Paul Lynde: There's Plenty of Tragedy Behind That Grin." *Sarasota Herald Tribune,* December 31, 1972: 15.

"Paul Lynde Arrested." *The Calgary Herald.* January 13, 1978: C7.

"Paul Lynde Dies, Wit on Hollywood Squares TV Show." *The Hour.* Norfolk, CT, January 12, 1982, 6.

"Paul Lynde Doing the Weather." WSPD-TV, Toledo 1978, Videoholic PRIME, YouTube. December 23, 2012. Videoclip. June 21, 2013. *www.youtube.com/watch?vNX_igvcBICc*

"Paul Lynde: Recently Released." Vinyl LP. mono j; Columbia Records CL1534 1960.

"Paul Lynde Took Time for Others." *The Bryon Times,* January 14, 1982.

"Paul Lynde was Voted the Funniest Man of the Year." *Lakeland Ledger.* June, 1, 1975.

The Paul Lynde Story. *E! Mysteries and Scandals.* Produced by Alison Martino. YouTube. July 14, 2011. Season 3, episode 37. Video clip. *http://www.youtube.com/watch?v=w8zlLFafCZo.* March 3, 2011.

The Paul Lynde Halloween Special, S'more Entertainment, Hoysyl Productions, 1976. DVD.

"Pedestrians See Actor Fall To Death." *Saskatoon Star,* Phoenix July 20, 1965: 5.

Perkins, Richard. Telephone Interview. October 12, 2011.

Pike, Charles and Cummings Roy, "Midnight Visits Paul Lynde's Magnificent Beverly Hills Estate." *Mid-Night,* December 22, 1975: 16-17.

Pilato, Herbie J. *Twitch Upon a Star.* Taylor Publishing, Maryland 2012: 27, 85, 196, 241.

Queer Music Heritage: "Madame Spivey." Web. June 8, 2013. *www.queermusicheritage.com*

Raddata, Leslie."If He Ever Calms Down, He'll Be in Trouble." *TV Guide*, February 10-16, 1973: 25.

Rae, Charolette. Telephone Interview. April 2013.

Rice, Connie. Telephone Interview January 11, 2011.

Rivera, Chita. Telephone Interview. January 20, 2012.

Roberts, Les. Email interview. January 19, 2011.

Robinson, Rob and Boutwell, Ron. Book Production — *The Paul Lynde Show,* 1976.

Rosinangel. "*I am Heathcliff.*" YouTube." February 22, 2008. Video clip. November 2012.

Rothman, Seymour, "If You're Famous, Give Him a Sign." *Toledo Blade.* July 1, 1990: 1.

Scott, Veron. "Award Shows to go to the Networks." *St. Joseph Missouri Spotlight,* January 1977: 12.

Shadrack, Herb, cinema archives, 1797-Exclusive!-Interview-with-acclaimed-actor-Nehemiah-Persoff, October 29, 2013.

Slifka, Adrian, "TV's Zany Paul Lynde Heads List of Kenley's Summers Stars," *Youngstown Vindicator,* May 14 1978: B-10.

Ten Chimney's Foundation. Web. *http://www.tenchimneys.org/.* July 28, 2012.

The Tonight Show, starring Johnny Carson. NBC Studios, Burbank California, 1976. Produced by Fred De Cordova. April 30, 1976. DVD.

"Traces of Sex Stimulant Drug Found in Body of Paul Lynde." *The Montreal Gazette,* January 15, 1982: 19.

"250 Attend Lynde Funeral Services." *The Daily Sentinel,* January 15, 1982: 8.

TV Radio Talk, February 1973: 32, 33.

Weiss, Ray, "TV Game Show Gave Paul Lynde Recogntion," *Lakeland Ledger,* August 15, 1980: C-1.

Welds Nichol, Daphne. Telephone Interview. September 9, 2011.

White, Betty. Telephone Interview. August 7, 2013.

Wilkie, Jane. "That what's his name is a very funny fellow." *TV Guide.* July 19-25, 1969: 15-17.

Wilson Earl, "Paul Lynde to Grow Colony of Stars." *St Petersburg Times.* July 10, 1963: 6-D.

Wilson, Earl, "Lynde is Afraid to be Alone — on a Stage," *Milwaukee Sentinel,* April 3, 1975: 19.

Windeler Robert, "Paul Lynde Hates Hollywood, Where He Feels like a Round Peg In TV's Square Hole," *People Magazine,* September 1976.

"That's Funny! Laughs Scarce in Lynde Interview." *The Milwaukee Sentinel.* July 27, 1973: 19.

"Comic Paul Lynde, Sometimes Serious." January 27, 1973, Daytona Beach, *Morning Journal:* 3b.

Wilson, Steve., Florenski, Joe. *Center Square,* California, Advocate Books, 2005: 11, 40, 129, 157, 220.

Witbeck, Charles. "Cookies Crumble for Paul Lynde." *Pittsburgh Post-Gazette,* January 4, 1973.

Woodbury, Woody. Email Interview. June 15, 2011.

Index

Cathy Rudolph, author. PHOTO COURTESY OF
RYAN RUDOLPH

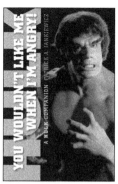

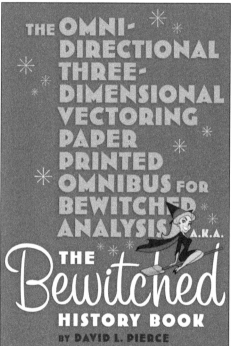
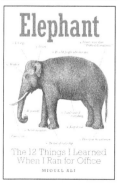

CPSIA information can be obtained
at www.ICGtesting.com
Printed in the USA
LVHW081253011021
699229LV00019B/109